"I have worked with this curriculum for more than a decade. I have seen the Spirit of God use this material to lead to the kind of spiritual reflection that encourages spiritual growth and draws one closer to God. I am certain it will be a spiritual catalyst for your group."

—DARRELL BOCK
research professor of New Testament Studies, professor of Spiritual Development and Culture, Dallas Theological Seminary

"The TRANSFORMING LIFE series involves spiritual formation elements that are individual and community-based, reflective and active—all working together in their proper time and manner. It is both scriptural and reality-based in unique and life-changing ways."

—BRAD SMITH
president, Bakke Graduate University

"An outstanding tool in the development of men and women of faith! I have personally used the principles and concepts of the earlier versions of this material for the past eight years; I can assure you that it is a time-tested, invaluable resource that I look forward to using in the years to come."

—DAN BOSCO
community life pastor, Vail Bible Church, Avon, Colorado

MINISTRY
Determining How I Serve

Center for Christian Leadership at Dallas Theological Seminary

NAVPRESS®

BRINGING TRUTH TO LIFE

OUR GUARANTEE TO YOU

We believe so strongly in the message of our books that we are making this quality guarantee to you. If for any reason you are disappointed with the content of this book, return the title page to us with your name and address and we will refund to you the list price of the book. To help us serve you better, please briefly describe why you were disappointed. Mail your refund request to: NavPress, P.O. Box 35002, Colorado Springs, CO 80935.

The Navigators is an international Christian organization. Our mission is to reach, disciple, and equip people to know Christ and to make Him known through successive generations. We envision multitudes of diverse people in the United States and every other nation who have a passionate love for Christ, live a lifestyle of sharing Christ's love, and multiply spiritual laborers among those without Christ.

NavPress is the publishing ministry of The Navigators. NavPress publications help believers learn biblical truth and apply what they learn to their lives and ministries. Our mission is to stimulate spiritual formation among our readers.

FOR A FREE CATALOG OF
NAVPRESS BOOKS & BIBLE STUDIES,
CALL 1-800-366-7788 (USA)
OR 1-416-499-4615 (CANADA)

Table of Contents

Acknowledgments   **7**

A Model of Spiritual Transformation   **9**

A Method for the Biblical Exercises   **17**

Determining How I Serve

    Session 1: Expanding Your Concept of Ministry   **19**
    Session 2: Ours for Others   **31**
    Session 3: Contexts of Ministry   **37**
    Session 4: Spirit-Directed Ministry   **43**
    Session 5: Ministry in the World   **51**
    Session 6: Ministry in the Church   **55**
    Session 7: Ministry in the Home   **59**
    Sessions 8–10: Life Vision Presentations   **63**
    Session 11: For the Glory of Christ   **67**

Life Vision   **75**

Leader's Guide   **127**

Notes   **141**

Acknowledgments

The TRANSFORMING LIFE series is based on a curriculum developed at Dallas Theological Seminary for its Spiritual Formation program, under the guidance of the Center for Christian Leadership. Hundreds of seminary students have benefited from this material, and now this adapted version makes it available to local churches and ministries.

This series would not have been possible without the contributions of many people and the support of Dallas Theological Seminary. The person primarily responsible for this series is Erik Petrik, senior pastor at Vail Bible Church in Vail, Colorado. As the director of the Spiritual Formation program in the late 1990s through 2000, Erik and his team developed the philosophy of this series and its fundamental components. The team he gathered included men and women with great spiritual insight and extensive ministry experience. It was primarily due to Erik's vision and the team's refining, researching, and writing that this series came to life.

In addition, the following persons made significant contributions: Terry Boyle, Barry Jones, Tim Lundy, Tom Miller, Elizabeth Nash, Jim Neathery, Kim Poupart, Kari Stainback, Troy Stringfield, and Monty Waldron. It was my great pleasure to work with each of them and experience the image of Christ in them.

Others who shaped the Spiritual Formation program at Dallas Seminary from the early 1990s are John Contoveros, Pete Deison, Martin Hironaga, David Kanne, Dr. Bill Lawrence, Brad Smith, and David Ward. Special appreciation goes to Pete Deison and David Kanne for their early contribution to what eventually became Life Story, and to Dr. Bill Lawrence, who gave the team the freedom to "think outside the box" when he was the executive director of the Center for Christian Leadership. Dr. Andrew Seidel, the current acting executive director, has continued to provide needed support through the process of revising the series for use in churches and ministries. Kerri Gupta contributed much time and energy cleaning up the manuscript. Thanks to her for her editing work.

Dallas Theological Seminary provided the context and the resources necessary for this series. Many students have given valuable feedback in the development at various stages. The support of the seminary administration has been invaluable. This series could not have come into being without its support.

WILLIAM G. MILLER
Resource Development Coordinator
Center for Christian Leadership
Dallas Theological Seminary

A Model of Spiritual Transformation

What's the first thing that comes to mind when you think of spiritual growth? Some picture a solitary individual meditating or praying. While that concept accurately portrays one aspect of Christian spirituality, it doesn't tell the whole story.

Three Aspects of Transformation

The issue of spiritual transformation is not new in the Christian faith. It has been a primary issue, though perhaps given different labels, throughout church history. From the time the Spirit of God descended upon the believers in Jerusalem, God has been transforming the souls of individual believers in the context of local Christian communities.

Preaching has never been and never will be the only element needed for the transformation of Christians into Christ's image. Nor are small-group Bible studies, personal Bible study, Sunday school classes, or even one-on-one discipleship sufficient for growing Christians when they focus solely on communicating biblical information. Therefore, a movement has grown that emphasizes transformation of the believer's inner and outer life and not just transformation of the intellect. Three broad approaches to spiritual transformation have developed.

Fellowship Model

One approach is to create fellowship opportunities. Churches develop structured settings for members to build relationships with others. They may launch small groups that meet in homes. They may convert their Sunday school classes into times of social engagement. These groups enable believers to be intimately involved in one another's lives. The fellowship model focuses on corporate prayer for one another, growth of interpersonal intimacy, and support for each other in times of need. This approach effectively connects believers within a church body.

Spiritual Disciplines Model

A second approach emphasizes disciplines such as meditation, prayer, fasting, and solitude. Such writers as Dallas Willard and Richard Foster have done excellent work on spiritual disciplines. This approach takes seriously the inner life and intimacy with God. However, when used in isolation, this approach can make people think spiritual transformation is a private matter. Even though the spiritual disciplines include communal elements (worship, service, and fellowship), some people treat the private exercises (silent retreats, journaling, meditating on Scripture, prayer, and fasting) as primary. That's a mistake.

Counseling Model

The third approach relies heavily on personal introspection. Christian counseling emphasizes areas of surrounding sin or personal character flaws that cause interpersonal problems or destructive behavior. Counseling seeks to understand the roots of such problems by looking at one's heritage and temperament. Usually in one-on-one interaction, the counselor probes for the root issues hidden beneath the surface problem. Discovering these deeper issues can shed light on a person's consistent failure to make wise choices. This approach focuses on identifying and dealing with those internal obstacles that prevent spiritual growth. Dealing with the issues is a key component in spiritual transformation.

The TRANSFORMING LIFE Model — An Integrated Approach

The three approaches are all valuable, but when taken alone they each have weaknesses. The fellowship model can fail to guide believers toward growth. The spiritual disciplines model can neglect to emphasize authentic and intimate Christian community, which is necessary for growth. The counseling model can fail to value the role that spiritual disciplines can have in growth. It also risks focusing on deficiencies so much that the person never benefits from the resources of God's grace. It can focus too intently upon the person's sin and failure and not enough on God's enabling power toward growth in holiness.

Therefore, TRANSFORMING LIFE brings in elements from all three approaches. The series tries to balance the inward and outward elements of spiritual transformation. Its theme is:

> Experiencing divine power through relationships;
> Striving together toward maturity in Christ.

We believe a particular context is essential to the transformation process. That context is authentic community in which people come to trust each other. Though one-on-one relationships can be effective, we believe that multiple relationships are more effective. While one individual can spur another toward growth, that one individual has limited gifts and abilities. Also, though we value the spiritual disciplines, we see them as means toward the end of complete transformation of the believer's inner and outer life. Disciplines aren't ends in themselves. Finally, we think believers need to seek greater understanding of sin's dynamic in their lives. They need to see potential blind spots or obstacles to their spiritual well-being and learn to deal with the root issues beneath their areas of struggle.

Our working definition of the Christian's transformation is:

> The process by which God forms Christ's character in believers by the ministry of the Spirit, in the context of community, and in accordance with biblical standards. This process involves the transformation of the whole person in thoughts, behaviors, and styles of relating with God and others. It results in a life of service to others and witness for Christ.

While the transformation process is an end in itself, the ultimate end is Christ's glory. He is the One adored by those who experience His presence and are transformed by Him. They, in turn, seek to exalt Him in the world.

Because each person is unique, God's formative process is unique for each. And though the Spirit of God is the One who transforms souls, each individual has personal responsibility in the process. Many spiritual disciplines can contribute, yet God is primarily concerned with transforming the whole person, not just patterns of behavior. For this reason, no one method (be it a traditional spiritual discipline or another method) is the single critical component.

TRANSFORMING LIFE depends solely on peer leadership. Groups don't need to be led by trained ministers. Leaders are more like facilitators—they don't need to have all the answers because group members learn from each other. The leader's role is to create an environment that fosters growth and encouragement.

Still, all small-group ministries need consistent coaching for the lay leaders. The group leaders need ministers and pastors to train and encourage them. A small-group ministry will raise all sorts of issues for leaders to deal with as people become honest about their lives in a trusting community. A group leader may need guidance about how to respond to a group member who shares that he has been having an e-mail "affair" and has not told his wife. Another may feel discouraged when group members drop out. Still another may wonder how to deal with two group members who are consistently angry with each other. It's important to provide support to those who take the risk to develop such an authentic environment for growth.

The Four Themes of This Series

Instead of aiming for competency in a set of skills or techniques, this series helps people identify the areas that must be developed in a believer's life. In other words, while it's necessary for a believer to know the "how-tos" of the Christian life, it's not sufficient. Knowing how to do personal Bible study and how to share Christ with others are praiseworthy skills. Developing these skills, however, is not the end goal but the means by which we live out who we are as new creatures in Christ. That's why this series addresses four critical components of the Christian life: identity, community, integrity, and ministry.

This series proposes that the Christian life involves:

> knowing your identity in Christ
> > *so that*
> you can make yourself known to others in a Christian community
> > *so that*
> you can pursue a lifetime of growth in the context of community
> > *so that*
> you are best equipped to glorify Christ by serving others.

Identity

To understand our need for transformation, we must understand who we are currently, both as individuals and as members of the body of Christ. Who we are has undoubtedly been shaped by our past. Therefore, we explore various aspects of our identity, such as our heritage and temperament. What do these tell us about who we are and what we value? The interaction during this study bonds us and builds trust among us. Our goal is not to analyze, criticize, or control each other, but it is to grow and affirm what God is doing in and through one another.

In *Identity*, we ultimately want group members to see themselves in light of their identity in Christ. However, many of the values we actually live out stem from such influences as temperament, family background, and culture. Not all of those values are contrary to our new identity in Christ. For example, the value one person places on honesty, which he learned from his parents, is affirmed by his identity in Christ.

It can take a long time—more than a lifetime allows—for the Spirit of God to transform our values to line up with our new identity in Christ. We cooperate with the Spirit when we reflect on what our values are and how well they line up with our identity in Christ as described in Scripture.

One of the most significant characteristics of our identity in Christ is that we are now part of the body of Christ. The Christian life cannot be lived in isolation.

Community

So, while talking about *my* place in Christ, I need to pay attention to *our* place in Christ as a community. Understanding our corporate identity in Christ is crucial for a healthy community transformation process. The *Community* study helps a group not only understand how a Christian community develops but also experience a growing sense of community.

In order to experience intimate community in the biblical sense, we must learn to reveal ourselves to others. We need to honestly, freely, and thoughtfully tell our stories. Our modern culture makes it easy for people to live isolated and anonymous lives. Because we and others move frequently, we may feel it's not worth the effort to be vulnerable in short-lived relationships. However, we desperately need to keep intentionally investing in significant relationships.

Real involvement in others' lives requires more than what the term *fellowship* has too often come to mean. Real involvement includes holding certain values in common and practicing a lifestyle we believe is noble, while appreciating that this lifestyle doesn't make us perfect. Rather, this lifestyle is a commitment to let God continue to spiritually form us.

Community includes a group exercise, "Life Story," that has been tremendously effective in building community and enhancing self-understanding. "Life Story" walks a person through the process of putting together a personal, creative presentation of the most formative relationships and experiences of his or her life. As people share their stories with each other, a deep level of trust and commitment grows.

Integrity

By the time a group has experienced *Identity* and *Community* together, members have built significant intimacy and trust. Now they're ready to pursue a harder step. It's the heart of our approach to spiritual transformation. Many believers greatly underestimate the necessity of intimacy and trust for successful growth in Christian holiness. But we must be able to share honestly those areas in which we need transformation. We can deal with deep issues of growth only in a community in which we're deeply known by others. We need others who have our best interests at heart. They must also be people we trust to hold sensitive issues in genuine confidence.

Why does the pursuit of Christian holiness need to occur in community? There are at least two reasons. First, we need accountability in the areas of sin with which we struggle. When we confess our struggles to a group, we become accountable to all of the members to press on toward growth. Because the group is aware of our sin, we can't hide it in darkness, where it retains a hold on our life and can make crippling guilt a permanent fixture in our walk. If we're struggling, we have not one but several people to lean on. In addition, the corporate, or group, setting increases the likelihood of support from someone else who has struggled in the same way. In one-on-one accountability, one person may not be able to relate well to the other's struggles. He or she may have different areas of struggle.

The second benefit of corporate pursuit of holiness is that without the encouragement and stimulus of other Christians, we're often blind to the ways in which we need to grow. In the counsel of many who care for us, there can be greater wisdom. If some believers are blind to being hospitable, the hospitality of another believer can spur them on to develop that quality in their own lives. If some never think about how to speak encouraging words, the encouraging speech of another can become contagious.

Ministry

With *Identity*, *Community*, and *Integrity* as a foundation, believers are prepared to discern how God wants them to serve in the body of Christ. "Where can I serve?" is not an optional question; every believer should ask it. Nor is this a matter simply for individual reflection. Rather, we can best discern where and how to serve while in community with people who know our past, interests, struggles, and talents. The community can affirm what they see in us and may know of opportunities to serve that we're unaware of.

How many terrific musicians are sitting in pews every Sunday because they lack the confidence to volunteer? Those gifted people might merely need others who know them well to encourage them to serve. Maybe someone's life story revealed that while growing up she played in a band. Someone might ask, "What have you done with that interest lately?"

The Layout of *Ministry*

Each session contains the following elements:
- *Session Aims* states a goal for you as an individual and one for the group.
- *Preparation* tells what assignment(s) you need to complete ahead of time in order to get the most out of the group. For this study, much of the preparation will involve completing "Life Vision" exercises. The "Life Vision" exercises can be found on pages 75-125.
- *Introduction* sets up the session's topic.
- *Content* provides material around which group discussions and exercises will focus. You should read the "Introduction" and "Content" sections before your group meeting so you'll be prepared to discuss them.

- *Conclusion* wraps up the session and sets the scene for the next one.
- *Assignment* lists "homework" to complete before the next session meeting.

In this way, each session includes all three aspects of transformation: personal introspection, spiritual disciplines, and the experience of God in relationships. Through all of these means, the Spirit of God will be at work in your life.

A Method for the Biblical Exercises

The biblical exercises will guide you through a self-study of a passage that relates to the session topic. You'll begin by making observations about the passage. Pay attention to the following categories:

Who?

Identify persons in the passage: the description of persons, the relationships between persons, and the condition of persons.

What?

Identify subjects in the passage: the issues or topics being addressed.

When?

Identify time in the passage: duration of time that passes and when the events occurred in relationship to one another.

Where?

Identify places in the passage: the descriptions of locations, the relationships of places to other places, and the relationships of persons to the places.

Why?

Identify purposes in the passage: the expressions of purpose by the author and/or the characters.

How?

Identify events in the passage: the descriptions of events unfolding, the relationships between events, and the order of events.

In *Living By the Book*, Dr. Howard Hendricks and William Hendricks identify six categories that aid the process of observation. They encourage readers to "look for things that are (1) emphasized, (2) repeated, (3) related, (4) alike, (5) unlike, or (6) true to life."[1]

After you make observations, you will interpret the passage. Interpretation involves determining what the main point of the passage is. Then you'll reflect on how the main point applies to your life. Be sure to ask for God's guidance in your reflection. After all, the purpose of Scripture is for God to speak to us and, as a result, for our lives to be transformed.

Expanding Your Concept of Ministry

Most of us think of ministry as the work done by pastors, missionaries, Christian conference speakers, or evangelists. We rarely think of work done by bankers, lawyers, engineers, or homemakers. We typically believe that those who get their paychecks from a church or other Christian organization are the ones who "do" ministry, while the rest of us are those to whom ministry is "done." In this session and throughout this study, we hope to change this common but faulty way of thinking. We want to expand your vision of ministry so that you come to view all you do, regardless of your occupation, as what it can and ought to be—ministry that glorifies God and influences other people.

Session Aims

Individual Aim: To consider a more holistic concept of ministry and how it relates to your everyday life.

Group Aim: To think together about ways in which group members' lives can become more ministry focused.

Preparation

Read *Session 1: Expanding Your Concept of Ministry*.

Complete the *Life Vision: Personal Inventory, Part I* exercise beginning on page 77.

Complete *Biblical Exercise: 1 Peter 4* beginning on page 25.

Introduction

> The idea that service to God should have only to do with a church altar, singing, reading, sacrifice, and the like is without doubt but the worst trick of the devil. How could the devil have led us more effectively astray than by the narrow conception that the service of God takes place only in the church and by works done therein. . . . The whole world could abound with services to the Lord . . . not only in churches but also in the home, kitchen, workshop, and field.[1]
>
> —Martin Luther

Content

The great reformer Martin Luther understood that ministry is more than just work done by pastors. Throughout this study, we will be using the term *ministry* in a way that is much broader than the way the term is usually used. Our definition of ministry is "the faithful service of God's people rendered unto God and others on His behalf to bring Him glory, build up His church, and reach out to His world." Let's look at this definition in more detail.

The Faithful Service of God's People

The Greek word in the New Testament that is often translated as "ministry" is *diakonia*. The basic meaning of this word is "service." It can refer to tasks as basic as waiting tables (see Acts 6:1), caring for the poor through monetary gifts (see 2 Corinthians 9:12), or proclaiming the gospel (see Acts 20:24). The term is not limited to the service of a select few appointed to particular offices within the church. In fact, the exact opposite is the case. Paul said that those who hold offices in the church are given gifts for the purpose of enabling all of God's people to do ministry:

> It was he who gave some to be apostles, some to be prophets, some to be evangelists, and some to be pastors and teachers, to prepare God's people for works of service [diakonia], so that the body of Christ may be built up. (Ephesians 4:11-12)

The leaders of the church are not the only ones doing the work of service or ministry. The leaders are given to the church for the purpose of preparing every member to do the ministry—to render service to the Lord, to the church, and to the world.

Rendered unto God

In our fast-paced, high-tech world, we often fail to recognize that God is intricately involved in the details of our lives. Yet not only is God involved in our humdrum routines, but He also wants us to be aware of and responsive to His presence:

> So whether you eat or drink or whatever you do, *do it all for the glory of God.* (1 Corinthians 10:31, emphasis added)

> And whatever you do, *whether in word or deed, do it all in the name of the Lord Jesus, giving thanks to God the Father through him.* (Colossians 3:17, emphasis added)

> Whatever you do, *work at it with all your heart, as working for the Lord, not for men, since you know that you will receive an inheritance from the Lord as a reward. It is the Lord Christ you are serving.* (Colossians 3:23-24, emphasis added)

Each of these exhortations from Paul's letters uses the phrase "whatever you do." This all-inclusive phrase points out that God wants to be prominent in our lives, in both the so-called "significant" things we do as well as the mundane things. We rarely think God is terribly concerned with our day-to-day activities in the boardroom, the classroom, or the laundry room, yet when our work is done "for the glory of God" (1 Corinthians 10:31), "in the name of the Lord Jesus" (Colossians 3:17), and "as working for the Lord" (Colossians 3:23), our work becomes an act of worship. Our work, however grand or trivial, becomes ministry.

And Others on His Behalf

The ultimate example of ministry is Jesus Christ Himself. In Paul's letter to the Philippians, he told his readers that their attitude toward each other "should be the same as that of Christ Jesus" (Philippians 2:5). Paul went on to describe the kind of attitude he was referring to:

> [Christ Jesus], being in very nature God,
>   did not consider equality with God something to be grasped,
> but made himself nothing,
>   taking the very nature of a servant,
>   being made in human likeness.
> And being found in appearance as a man,
>   he humbled himself
>   and became obedient to death—even death on a cross!
>   (Philippians 2:6-8)

Jesus set aside the glory due Him and took on the form of a slave. His entire life on earth, and ultimately His death on the cross, was others-oriented. Paul's admonition to the Philippians and to all of us as Christians is to imitate this others-orientation. This is particularly challenging in our culture, which is consumed with self.

For example, this cultural preoccupation often dominates our view of the way we make a living. We often think of our jobs in terms of the financial benefits they provide for us and our families. This isn't necessarily wrong, but we also ought to consider how our work can benefit others—either customers who benefit from our goods or services, or perhaps our coworkers, whose lives we can affect by serving them in times of need. If we are to imitate Jesus and thereby do the work of ministry to which we have all been called, we must learn to look at life with an others-orientation in our workplaces, our homes, our churches, and every other arena.

To Bring Him Glory

The Westminster Shorter Catechism begins, "Man's chief end is to glorify God and to enjoy Him forever."[2] If this confession is true of all of humanity collectively and of each human being individually, then it should also be true of the pieces that make up the whole of our lives—from the way we parent to the way we play, from the time we spend "on the clock" to the time we spend at the dinner table.

In the passage from 1 Corinthians quoted earlier, Paul said that activities as simple as eating and drinking can and should be done "for the glory of God" (10:31). God is glorified when we do anything with thankfulness, integrity, and our whole hearts. Thankfulness comes from a recognition that all we have and all we are able to accomplish comes from God. We fail to be thankful and to glorify God when we act and think as though we are self-sufficient rather than utterly dependent on Him.

Likewise, we live with integrity when our thoughts and actions are consistent with God's ethical intentions for His people. We compromise our integrity when our desires conflict with God's intentions.

Wholeheartedness means focusing on giving our best in all we do, not for the accolades we might receive but out of a desire to do what we do as unto Christ (see Colossians 3:23). As we go about our daily tasks with thankfulness, integrity, and wholeheartedness, God sees and is pleased. Others see and His reputation is enhanced—He is glorified. When we seek to glorify God in all we do, all we do becomes ministry.

Build Up His Church

Each of us has a special responsibility and has been uniquely gifted to minister to others. In his book *Redeeming the Routines*, theologian Robert Banks likens the coming together of believers in a local church to the gathering of children for a birthday party. Everyone brings a gift; the only difference is that in the church, the gifts aren't for one person but for everyone.[3]

The New Testament makes it clear that all who have been born of the Spirit have been endowed with a spiritual gift (or perhaps multiple gifts). The main point of the New Testament discussion of spiritual gifts is that each of us, as individual members of the body, needs the contribution of the entire body and conversely the entire body needs the contribution of each individual member. Each of us in the body of Christ has needs, and each has something to contribute to others' needs.

As we come to see that as Christians we are all called to do ministry, we ought to reflect upon how God has designed and gifted us to build up His church. We will visit this issue of design and giftedness again in later sessions.

And Reach Out to His World

In the book of Genesis, God gave a set of covenant promises to Abraham and his descendants. He promised that He would bless them and that through them He would bless "all peoples on earth" (Genesis 12:3; 28:14). Throughout Old Testament times, God wanted His people to be a missionary people who would visibly demonstrate to the pagan world around them that the Lord alone was the one true God. As God's beloved people, Israel had both a blessing and a purpose—to make God known to the world. Psalm 67 captures these two themes of blessing and purpose:

> May God be gracious to us and bless us
> and make his face shine upon us,
> that your ways may be known on earth,
> your salvation among all nations.
> May the peoples praise you, O God;
> may all the peoples praise you.
> May the nations be glad and sing for joy,
> for you rule the peoples justly
> and guide the nations of the earth.
> May the peoples praise you, O God;
> may all the peoples praise you.
> Then the land will yield its harvest,
> and God, our God, will bless us.
> God will bless us,
> and all the ends of the earth will fear him.

These same themes of blessing and purpose apply to Christians as well. We have been richly blessed through Christ and have been given a responsibility to spread the good news of His life, death, and resurrection. This is not a job reserved for a select few; it is God's purpose for every Christian. Certainly God has uniquely designed some to take the message of Christ to people in the far reaches of the world, but all of us have our own "mission fields" in our homes, neighborhoods, places of employment, and the like. It is our responsibility to spread the gospel with our words and live out the gospel with our lives.

Conclusion

In his book *The Other Six Days*, R. Paul Stevens writes,

> Throughout most of its history the church has been composed of two categories of people, those who are ministers and those who are not. Ministry has been defined as what the pastor does, not in terms of being servants of God and God's purposes in the market-place, the church, the home, the school or professional office. Going into "the Lord's work" means becoming a pastor or a missionary, not being coworkers with God in his creating, sustaining, redeeming and consummating work both in the church and in the world.[4]

Our goal in this session and throughout this study is to present a different view of ministry, one more consistent with the teaching of Scripture. We do "the Lord's work" when we do whatever we do for the glory of God and the good of others.

Biblical Exercise: 1 Peter 4

Read 1 Peter 4:1-11. Also, review "A Method for the Biblical Exercises" beginning on page 17.

Observation — "What Do I See?"

1. Who are the persons (including God) in the passage? What is the condition of those persons?

2. What subjects did Peter discuss in the passage? What did he assert?

3. Note the sequence in which Peter made these assertions. (You might number them in order.)

4. What did Peter emphasize? Are there repeated ideas and themes? How are the various parts related?

5. Why did Peter write this passage? (Did he say anything about ways he expected the reader to change after reading it?)

Interpretation Phase 1 — **"What Did It Mean Then?"**

1. Coming to Terms — Are there any words in the passage that you don't understand? Write down anything you found confusing about the passage.

2. Finding Where It Fits — What clues does the Bible give about the meaning of this passage?

   - Immediate Context (the passage being studied)

   - Remote Context (passages that come before and after the one being studied)

3. Getting into Their Sandals — An Exercise in Imagination

   - What are the main points of this passage? Summarize or write an outline of it.

- What do you think the recipients of the letter were supposed to take from this passage? How did God, inspiring Peter to write this letter, want this passage to impact readers?

Interpretation Phase 2 — **"What Does It Mean Now?"**

1. What is the timeless truth in the passage? In one or two sentences, write down what you learned about God from 1 Peter 4.

2. How does that truth work today?

Application — **"What Can I Do to Make This Truth Real?"**

1. What can I do to make it real for myself?

2. For my family?

3. For my friends?

4. For the people who live near me?

5. For the rest of the world?

Assignment

Read *Session 2: Ours for Others*.

Complete the *Life Vision: Personal Inventory, Part II* exercise beginning on page 83.

Ours for Others

In session 1, we saw that all Christians ought to be ministers and that all we do, when done in a certain way, can qualify as ministry. In this session, we will explore the New Testament concept of *calling*. We will discover that God, in His sovereign authorship of our lives, has been molding and shaping us from birth to be effective ministers. God has uniquely crafted and gifted us and brought us through a specific set of experiences and relationships. He wants us to draw on all of these to make a distinct impact on the world around us.

Session Aims

Individual Aim: To understand what a personal calling is.

Group Aim: To discuss the concept of calling and its implications for us.

Preparation

Read *Session 2: Ours for Others*.

Complete the *Life Vision: Personal Inventory, Part II* exercise beginning on page 83.

Introduction

Many people say that they aren't exactly sure what a calling from God is but that they're pretty sure they haven't received one: "Aren't there some people who are 'called' to ministry and others who aren't? Don't those who become pastors and missionaries go into those ministries because they have received some kind of divine calling?" To answer these questions, we need to carefully examine the way the language of calling is used in the New Testament. When we do so, we discover that all Christians are called.

Content

Although New Testament writers occasionally used the word *calling* to refer to the selection of certain individuals for special service to the Lord ("Set apart for me Barnabas and Saul for the work to which I have called them" Acts 13:2), this is not the primary way *calling* is used. The fact that the term is used in this way so infrequently should teach us that we shouldn't focus on who has or hasn't received this kind of divine calling. Instead we should be concerned with the way calling applies to all of us as Christians. The primary way New Testament writers speak of calling is *to refer to a person's salvation.* In this sense, every true Christian has responded positively to the divine call to become children of God through Christ. Consider these verses:

> *God,* who has called you into fellowship with his Son *Jesus Christ our Lord, is faithful. (1 Corinthians 1:9, emphasis added)*

> *He* called you to this salvation *through our gospel, so that you may possess the glory of our Lord Jesus Christ. (2 Thessalonians 2:14, NET, emphasis added)*

> *And the God of all grace,* who called you to his eternal glory in Christ, *after you have suffered a little while, will himself restore you and make you strong, firm and steadfast. (1 Peter 5:10, emphasis added)*

These are just a few of the many verses that speak of our salvation in terms of calling; therefore, we shouldn't think that some Christians are called and others aren't.

But it's true that we're called to more than salvation alone. We are also all *called to be a part of a community.* In our individualistic North American context, we often interpret the Bible in individualistic ways, but at the heart of the New Testament understanding of Christianity is community. In fact, each of the verses quoted above is addressed not to individuals but to a group. Our call to salvation is a call to identify with and to share in the eternal destiny of the community of those who place their faith in Jesus Christ.

A third way we're called is to *a life of obedience and service* that is "worthy of the calling you have received" (Ephesians 4:1; 2 Thessalonians 1:11).

R. Paul Stevens sums up the ways the New Testament speaks of calling as *belonging, being,* and *doing.* He writes,

> The call of God is threefold. First there is the call to *belong to God.* Thus persons without identities or "names," who are homeless waifs in the universe, become children of God and members of the family of God. . . . This is the call to discipleship. Second, there is the call *to be God's people* in life, a holy people that exists for the praise of his glory in all aspects of life in the church and in the world. This is expressed in sanctification; it is the call to holiness. Third, there is the call to *do God's work,* to enter into God's service to fulfill his purposes in both the church and in the world. This involves gifts, talents, ministries, occupations, roles, work and mission—the call to service.[1]

This third aspect of God's call is our focus in this study, but we need to understand that all three aspects are inseparably bound up in God's one call for us. He has called all of us to belong to Him, be His people in life, and do His work.

In his description of the call to do God's work, Stevens mentions things such as gifts, talents, ministries, occupations, roles, work, and mission. God wants us to see all of these as resources for serving Him. He has given us our gifts and talents in order for us to use them for His purposes. He has placed us in our occupations so we can minister for Him there. He has also brought us through experiences and relationships to shape us into the kind of people He can use to meet others' needs.

On this aspect of calling, Os Guinness writes, "Calling is the truth that God has called us to himself so decisively that *everything we are, everything we do, and everything we have* is invested with a special devotion, dynamism, and direction lived out as a response to his summons and service."[2] He goes on to say, "We have nothing that was not given to us. Our gifts are ultimately God's, and we are only 'stewards'—responsible for prudent management of property that is not our own. This is why our gifts are always *ours for others,* whether in the community of Christ or the broader society outside, especially the neighbor in need."[3]

We often hear sermons on being "good stewards" by giving our financial resources to God. But as Guinness points out, good stewardship involves much more than that. It involves using "everything we are, everything we do, and everything we have" for God's work. As an example, consider Paul's words to the Corinthians:

> Praise be to the God and Father of our Lord Jesus Christ, the Father of compassion and the God of all comfort, who comforts us in all our troubles, so that *we can comfort those in any trouble with the comfort we ourselves have received from God.* (2 Corinthians 1:3-4, emphasis added)

Here Paul told the Corinthians that part of God's purpose in comforting them in their difficulties was to equip them to be His instruments to do the same for others. Sometimes our deepest sources of pain can become our deepest resources for ministry if we make those experiences available to others. Again, all we are and have is "ours for others." Gifts and talents, joys and sorrows, strengths and weaknesses, successes and failures, time and money—God has sovereignly allowed all of these into our lives and wants us to use them as resources for ministry.

For example, Jack's tragic loss of his mother when he was a little boy and his wife when he was an old man gave him an acute ability to speak about pain. His years as a hardened atheist and his keen God-given intellect made him one of Christianity's great intellectual defenders. His vivid imagination, years of literary study, and gift for telling stories enabled him to write wonderful children's books such as *The Horse and His Boy*, *The Voyage of the Dawn Treader*, and *The Lion, the Witch and the Wardrobe*. God's authorship of the life of C. S. ("Jack") Lewis made Lewis one of the most influential Christian writers of the twentieth century.

Lewis's temperament and gifting, along with his unique set of formative experiences and relationships, enabled him to leave his mark on the world. He was never "called" to become a pastor, never trained at a seminary, and never left the security of home to become a missionary, yet his ministry has affected hundreds of thousands of people around the world because what he had he made available to God. And God used him mightily.

Conclusion

We may never have the same fame or influence that C. S. Lewis had, but each of us can and should make a mark on the world around us. God has called us to Himself, called us into community, and called us to do His work in the world. Each of us has a unique contribution to make that is shaped by God's sovereign design and providential guidance.

Assignment

Read *Session 3: Contexts of Ministry.*

Complete the *Life Vision: Roles and Needs* exercise beginning on page 89.

Contexts of Ministry

Having established that we should use all we have in serving others, we will now turn our attention to where this ministry will occur.

Throughout your day, you live in various contexts. Perhaps you begin your day talking with your husband and children over breakfast. Then you head to the office, where you interact with coworkers and fulfill your tasks. Over lunch you meet an old friend from college. After work you stop by the high school to pick up your son from band practice and have a conversation on the way home about his day. Maybe you see a friend at the grocery store or stop to greet your neighbor. After dinner you attend a meeting held by the city to discuss zoning for a new neighborhood school. Each day, you encounter a variety of contexts, or settings, in which you can have a ministry mindset when interacting with others.

In this session, you will be introduced to three broad categories of contexts in which you can minister: the world, the church, and the home.

Session Aims

Individual Aim: To identify the needs of others and the contexts in which you can serve others.

Group Aim: To consider the particular contexts in which each group member can minister.

Preparation

Read *Session 3: Contexts of Ministry*.

Complete the *Life Vision: Roles and Needs* exercise beginning on page 89.

Introduction

How often do you lie in bed at night and think, *What did I accomplish today?* Some people ask themselves this question at the end of each day. Others may ask themselves, *What do I need to get done tomorrow?* Still others reach the end of the day so exhausted that they don't have the energy to ask themselves anything.

Perhaps a better question to ask at the end of the day is, *How well did I depend on God in my ministry to others today?* As we move through our typical daily routines, we interact with our brothers and sisters in Christ and with those who aren't Christians. In all of these interactions, we should seek to have an others-oriented, ministry mindset.

Peter urged his readers to lay down their lives for the sake of others, for those both in the church and in the larger world:

> *Now that you have purified yourselves by obeying the truth so that you have sincere love for your brothers, love one another deeply, from the heart. (1 Peter 1:22)*

> *Maintain good conduct among the non-Christians, so that though they now malign you as wrongdoers, they may see your good deeds and glorify God when he appears. (1 Peter 2:12, NET)*

Notice that Peter emphasized both loving fellow Christians and behaving excellently among those outside the church. Later in Peter's letter, he again implored his audience to live out their faith both in the public arena and in the community of faith:

> *Honor all people, love the family of believers, fear God, honor the king. (1 Peter 2:17, NET)*

Peter said, "Honor all people," whether they are coworkers, employers, family members, or perfect strangers. Jesus' story of the good Samaritan (see Luke 10:25-37) may have been ringing in Peter's ears as he wrote the phrase "Honor all people." Jesus told that story in response to the question "Who is my neighbor?" His story makes it clear that our neighbor is anyone whom God brings across our path. We need to show honor to everyone

God brings into our lives, whether they are in authority over us, serving us, or simply someone we randomly encounter.

The broad scope of Peter's instructions has significant implications for all of our interactions with other people, regardless of the context. In this session, we will focus on three common contexts.

Content

The three main contexts for ministry are the world, the church, and the home. The world, as we will use the term, refers to the work we do and the interactions we have outside an explicitly Christian context and with people other than our families. This includes our jobs, our neighborhoods, our favorite restaurant, and our children's PTA meetings. The church represents not only things done at a church but also those things we do specifically with and for other believers (the term *church* in the New Testament is never used of a building but always of a gathering of believers). The home will refer to what we do with our families. These are all contexts in which we should fulfill our calling to minister.

In each context, we have multiple roles. For example, in the world, you might be an electrician, a neighbor, and a Little League baseball coach. In the church, you might be a deacon, an accountability partner, and a financial supporter. In the home, you might be a wife, a mother, and a daughter. Reflecting on the roles you play in each context will help you understand that everything you do can be an act of ministry.

The World

Our roles in the world provide many opportunities for ministry. The role in which most of us spend the majority of our waking hours is our occupation, our job. In our job, we typically interact with both believers and unbelievers. In this role, we aren't financially compensated to be Christian witnesses (unless, for example, we work on a church staff). We are compensated to do a task or manage people. Even full-time parents or homemakers, who don't have paying jobs, interact with store clerks, school employees, and other children's families. The way we fulfill our responsibilities in our job is part of the ministry to which we have been called.

Consider the following Scripture:

> For we are to God the aroma of Christ among those who are being
> saved and those who are perishing. To the one we are the smell of death;
> to the other, the fragrance of life. And who is equal to such a task? . . .
> Not that we are competent in ourselves to claim anything for ourselves,
> but our competence comes from God. He has made us competent as
> ministers of a new covenant—not of the letter but of the Spirit; for the
> letter kills, but the Spirit gives life. (2 Corinthians 2:15-16; 3:5-6)

An attitude of service and a willingness to lay aside our own interests for
the interests of others should pervade our entire life. In this way, our jobs
will be contexts for ministry. Ministry in that context involves both the
way we interact with others and the way we accomplish our tasks.

We should do our work with a commitment to excellence. Adam and Eve
were created to labor in Eden. While it was an entirely pleasant labor
before their fall, God intended them to do their work with excellence.
Likewise, God gives each of us labor to perform with excellence. Whether
that involves changing diapers, writing computer software, plowing a field,
managing a marketing team, or framing a house, all of our responsibilities
ought to be performed with our utmost effort and concentration.

The manner in which we accomplish tasks is not our only concern if we
want to have an attitude of ministry at the workplace. The Christian
worker shouldn't have an "accomplish at all costs" attitude. The way we
interact with others also counts. After all, our witness to those who don't
share our beliefs and work ethic—and our example to fellow believers who
do—is related to how we love more than to anything else. Love should be
our chief characteristic (see 1 John 4:8). Our ministry at work involves
both working as if we were working for the Lord and relating well with
others.

The Church

While many of us spend most of our waking hours doing our job, our workplace is not the only arena for ministry. Just as every believer should live a
life of ministry in the world, every believer should also serve others in the
church. While there is no sharp distinction between these two, it's

important to keep in mind that we have a responsibility to give of ourselves in both contexts.

What does ministry in the church mean? It is ministry performed explicitly as a representative of Christ with and for other believers. It includes such things as leading a small group, being an usher, working at a Christian homeless shelter, doing evangelism on a short-term mission trip in Asia, providing refreshments for a small group, serving on a cleanup committee for the youth group gatherings, and organizing a Christian businessperson's luncheon.

Almost every church leader needs more laborers. There are more great ideas for how believers can serve each other and their communities than there are laborers to implement them. If you have been ministered to but have not yet ministered in the church, now is the time to jump in and begin. This study will help you think about where to start. If you have been ministering in the church, it will help you explore how you serve so that your service will fit your giftedness. The body of Christ needs each believer to serve in just the way God has gifted him or her—and to do so with excellence.

The Home

The most important context of ministry is with one's own family members. There is no higher calling to other people than to one's own family. While your roles in your job and church are important, your role as a member of your family takes precedence. Ministry in a job or church should never make you neglect the calling to minister to your own family. Jesus demonstrated this principle when He provided for His mother by charging John with her care—even while He hung on the cross (see John 19:25-27).

Conclusion

The purpose of this study is to help you see your entire life—your job, roles in the church, relationships within your family, and every other area of daily life—as ministry. We have been called to love just as Christ loved. That doesn't necessarily mean we are to begin a traveling ministry like Jesus. Rather, we are to love others in all the contexts in which God has placed us. We are ministers of new life in Christ. Let us walk by the Spirit in an all-pervasive life of ministry.

Assignment

Read *Session 4: Spirit-Directed Ministry*.

Complete the *Life Vision: Ministry Vision Statement* exercise beginning on page 97.

Complete *Biblical Exercise: John 15* beginning on page 46.

Spirit-Directed Ministry

In session 3, we saw that ministry should be an all-pervasive attitude in the world, the church, and the home. This session will focus on the power that enables us to live out an attitude of ministry in all areas of our lives. That power is the Holy Spirit of God. We must seek God's wisdom and strength through His Spirit in order to develop a vision for ministry and live it out in every context.

Session Aims

Individual Aim: To establish a ministry vision for each context in dependence upon the Spirit.

Group Aim: To encourage one another by listening to each group member's ministry vision and offering feedback.

Preparation

Read *Session 4: Spirit-Directed Ministry*.

Complete the *Life Vision: Ministry Vision Statement* exercise beginning on page 97.

Complete the *Biblical Exercise: John 15* exercise on page 46.

Introduction

Have you ever found yourself in a situation at work that made you completely confused about how to respond? You may have asked yourself, *What does it look like to love my boss?* or *How do I make an ethical choice when all I seem to have available are unethical alternatives?* You may face similar challenges at church. A kid in the youth group shares something with you in confidence, and you aren't sure whether you need to address it with one of the pastors. The church leadership makes a decision that you think adversely affects your ministry as a Sunday school teacher. Should you respond? If so, how?

If you have a relationship with God through faith in Christ, you have without a doubt experienced the guidance of the Spirit of God. Even the moment in which you placed your faith in Christ for the forgiveness of sin was a moment of responding to wisdom revealed by the Holy Spirit. You have probably also experienced many moments since then in which you have been led by the Spirit, whether you knew it at the time or only upon later reflection. It's helpful to reflect on those times in order to remind yourself of God's faithfulness. If you seek His guidance, wisdom, and strength, He will provide.

Content

Jesus compared the Spirit's regenerating work to the wind. "The wind blows wherever it pleases. You hear its sound, but you cannot tell where it comes from or where it is going. So it is with everyone born of the Spirit" (John 3:8). The Holy Spirit works in individuals, drawing them to the Father. Every believer is indwelled, baptized, and sealed by the Spirit. As Jesus pointed out, this work is beyond human control. Those of us who are God's children must humbly recognize His work in our lives. Our salvation depends on the Spirit's work.

And we are still in a state of dependence: "Those who are led by the Spirit of God are sons of God" (Romans 8:14). We no longer walk according to the flesh but should make all of our decisions under the leadership of the Spirit. Sometimes the Spirit moves in direct ways. He makes abundantly clear the course we are to take. The most common way He does this is through the Word. Have you ever been going through your day and suddenly a Bible passage comes to mind that relates to the circumstances of that moment and tells you how to respond?

Consider an example of a father who takes his little boy to the beach. The son says, "How many grains of sand do you think there are?" The father is spontaneously reminded by the Spirit of Psalm 139:17-18. He responds, "There sure are more than we can count, aren't there? Did you know that God has more thoughts about us than there are grains of sand?" The boy learns about God's great love in a way that is relevant to his experience. That is a simple example of how the Spirit of God uses the Word of God.

The Spirit also uses the counsel of others in guiding us. Have you ever been discouraged and experienced the power of encouraging words from a fellow believer who motivated you to persevere in godliness?

Consider two coworkers who go out to lunch together. One is a longtime employee of the company and the other just joined the staff. Over their meal, the longtime employee discovers that the newcomer is also a believer. The newcomer shares about her struggle as a Christian in the company. The veteran tells about her early struggles at the company and how she has come to be respected for her faith and her contribution as a dependable worker. The newcomer leaves lunch with a renewed sense of dependence upon Christ at her job and a sense of hope that she can persevere through the present trials. That's how the Spirit can provide strength and wisdom through the counsel of others. The Spirit of God indwells fellow believers and ministers through them.

At other times, the Spirit causes our hearts to burn with passion for a cause in God's kingdom. We can think of nothing else and experience restlessness until we can pursue the course He laid before us. Sometimes the Spirit inspires us to the core of our being with a passion for serving others who have some particular need.

Consider the example of a stay-at-home mom who meets a single, teenage mom at the park. After the interaction, the older mom becomes burdened for teen mothers. She decides to start a ministry of support and encouragement for teen mothers.

The Spirit is not bound to work in one way or another and may use a combination of the Word, counsel, and the desires of our heart to guide us in ministry.

Conclusion

The Spirit's guidance leads us into ministry and gives us strength and wisdom in ministry. Because each person's life is unique, including the roles held and circumstances present, individuals need a great deal of wisdom to discern how to live with a ministry attitude. The changing life circumstances that we all face give us the opportunity to depend on the Spirit afresh every day.

In addition to giving support for daily decisions, the Spirit can also help us establish a vision for ministry that can broaden our sense of purpose and direction. In the next three sessions, you will refine your ministry vision and develop a plan for ministry in the world, the church, and the home. Seek the Spirit's wisdom in this process.

Biblical Exercise: John 15

Read John 15:1-17. Also, review "A Method for the Biblical Exercises" beginning on page 17.

Observation — "What Do I See?"

1. Who are the persons (including God) in the passage? What is the condition of those persons?

2. What subjects did Jesus discuss in the passage? What did He assert?

3. Note the sequence in which Jesus made these assertions. (You might number them in order.)

4. What did Jesus emphasize? Are there repeated ideas and themes? How are the various parts related?

5. Why did Jesus say what He said? (Did He say anything about ways He expected people to change as a result of hearing that?)

Interpretation Phase 1 — **"What Did It Mean Then?"**

1. Coming to Terms—Are there any words in the passage that you don't understand? Write down anything you found confusing about the passage.

2. Finding Where It Fits—What clues does the Bible give about the meaning of this passage?

   • Immediate Context (the passage being studied)

   • Remote Context (passages that come before and after the one being studied)

3. Getting into Their Sandals—An Exercise in Imagination

   • What are the main points of this passage? Summarize or write an outline of the passage.

- What do you think the readers of this passage were supposed to take from it? How did God, inspiring John to write this passage, want it to impact those who read it?

Interpretation Phase 2 — **"What Does It Mean Now?"**

1. What is the timeless truth in the passage? In one or two sentences, write down what you learned about God from John 15.

2. How does that truth work today?

Application — "What Can I Do to Make This Truth Real?"

1. What can I do to make this truth real for myself?

2. For my family?

3. For my friends?

4. For the people who live near me?

5. For the rest of the world?

Assignment

Read *Session 5: Ministry in the World.*

Complete the *Life Vision: Action Steps, The World* exercise beginning on page 113.

Ministry in the World

In session 3, we introduced a distinction between ministry in the world, the church, and the home. We will now discuss ministry action steps for each area. Action steps vary, depending on our season of life and the details of our context, so each of us needs to reevaluate our vision periodically.

Session Aims

Individual Aim: To reevaluate your vision for ministry in the world and identify action steps to attain it.

Group Aim: To encourage and support each other in the process of developing action steps for ministry in the world.

Preparation

Read *Session 5: Ministry in the World.*

Complete the *Life Vision: Action Steps, The World* exercise beginning on page 113.

Introduction

In an autobiographical essay, novelist Walter Wangerin reflects on Paul's words in 1 Corinthians 13:11. Wangerin says, "When I was a child I spoke as a child, I understood as a child. When I became a man I put away childish things, but the man I became was shaped in childhood, and that shape remains forever."[1] Many forces have shaped you into the man or woman you have become.

In this session, you will look at some of the forces that have shaped you with an eye toward your ministry within the world. While most of this session emphasizes a workplace setting, ministry in the world encompasses a larger scope. Your "world" encompasses your PTA, neighborhood preschool playgroups, a homeowners association, city recreation leagues, social clubs, stores, and anywhere else you gather with unbelievers.

Content

Think of your vision as a picture of what you want your ministry to look like. For example, you may want a ministry of mentoring your team of analysts. In order to minister to the people on your team, you will take specific steps to attain that vision. You may commit to having lunch with each person on the team twice a month. You may keep a file on all individuals with notes of previous conversations and questions you want to ask them. You may help them come up with plans for their personal development. You may periodically invite them to your home. These are the kinds of action steps you will record in your "Life Vision" exercise for this session.

In addition to action steps, you also need to think about obstacles you'll face as you pursue your vision. Ministry vision isn't pie-in-the-sky dreams; it's a commitment to demonstrate Christian love and ethics to those with whom you come in contact. Knowing yourself well lets you understand the challenges you'll face in living out your ministry vision. Remembering past experiences in which you struggled with an issue can make you aware of how temptations tended to trip you up. Awareness of those past experiences can help you overcome those temptations today.

For instance, if you have consistently been drawn into cynical gossip in the break room about your coworkers, you may need to avoid the break room or be more prepared to restrain yourself from gossiping. Maybe each time you go into the break room, you can commit to an attitude of prayer, seeking God's moment-by-moment guidance for what you say. The obstacles section of your "Life Vision" exercise is a good place to note temptations you'll face.

Time is the top obstacle on many people's lists. We're so overwhelmed with responsibilities that we can't imagine adding one more thing. Be realistic and gentle with yourself. What *can* you do? If you don't have time to have lunch with every team member twice a month, could you make time to do so with each team member *once* a month? Know your limits, but let God stretch you.

To live according to your ministry vision, you'll need to pay deliberate attention to it each day. You must daily seek God's guidance and strength to live it. When you fail to do so, seek forgiveness first from God and then from others, if necessary. For example, if you are committed to encouraging your employees, you may have to apologize for discouraging or cynical comments. Don't give up on your ministry vision simply because you experience failure. Failure is defined not by moments when you live contrary to your vision but by ceasing to be committed to it altogether. In many "world" settings, living out godly character is a daunting task. Many workplaces provide no incentive for godliness; some offer incentive for ungodliness. Believers can't expect godly character from those who have no dynamic, life-changing relationship with a holy God. Don't expect unbelievers to embrace the lifestyle God has led you to embrace. Rather, seek to live a holy life in their presence for His glory.

Conclusion

In some ways, your past experience and personal makeup may help you be Christ's witness in your world. In other ways, you may feel those things create overwhelming challenges for your effectiveness as a witness. Yet in both your strengths and weaknesses, God wants you to walk through your day in relationship with and reliance on Him, with a heart that intends to glorify Him rather than yourself.

Assignment

Read *Session 6: Ministry in the Church*.

Complete the *Life Vision: Action Steps, The Church* exercise beginning on page 117.

Ministry in the Church

In session 5, you thought about your ministry vision in the world. In this session, you'll reflect on your vision for ministry in the church and the action steps you need to take in order to accomplish it. Even if you've never been involved in Christian service, you can start thinking about it. In light of your personal resources and the needs you know of, what kind of ministry should you be involved with? How do you go about getting involved? Whether you are refining your vision for an existing ministry or just getting started, this session will help you.

Session Aims

Individual Aim: To reevaluate your vision for ministry in the church and identify action steps that will help you attain it.

Group Aim: To encourage and support each other in the process of developing action steps for ministry in the church.

Preparation

Read *Session 6: Ministry in the Church*.

Complete the *Life Vision: Action Steps, The Church* exercise beginning on page 117.

Introduction

Most Christian organizations have an established ministry vision that guides what they do. In your occupation, you may have to establish a ministry vision that the organization doesn't embrace, but in a Christian organization, the established vision often gives you enough guidance in your role there. Your church's vision for small-group leaders, for example, may be completely adequate for guiding you as a group leader. Embrace that vision, and seek to serve consistently with it.

It's still helpful, though, to reflect on your personal ministry vision. You may find that God convicts you to embrace additional biblical principles. For instance, in a ministry to the homeless, the main goal may be to meet physical needs. While the organization may not emphasize evangelism, you may feel that sharing your faith is a priority that God has put on your heart. As long as you make sure that the way you live out that vision is acceptable to the leadership, you ought to remain committed to it.

Content

The difference between laboring in a Christian organization and laboring in your occupation is that in the former one, you explicitly represent Christ and His church. In your occupation, others may or may not think of you as a Christian, depending on how well they know you. In Christian service, others can rightly assume you represent the Christian message, the Christian community, and Christ Himself. When you teach a Sunday school lesson for a group of fourth-grade kids, those kids and their parents expect that your character and attitude will reflect the character and attitude of Christ. You are expected to love those children and teach them about Christ and His commands.

On the one hand, living out a ministry vision in a Christian organization can be easier than doing so at work. People have a deeper sense of responsibility and often built-in accountability to one another. While your coworker at the office has no vested interest in whether you live out biblical principles at the office, your partner in leading the youth group, as well as the parents, will question you if your behavior gives a poor example for the kids.

On the other hand, it's easy for Christian service to slip into a status quo. You may think your service as an usher amounts to showing up and going through the motions. But if you take your service seriously, you will check your attitude to make sure your heart is bent toward loving fellow church members and guests. You might pray, for example, that the Lord will use your ushering to encourage someone who is downcast. This way of ministering is far harder to sustain week in and week out.

You will always minister imperfectly. You will never achieve perfect consistency in living out your vision, especially if you prayerfully continue to reevaluate and refine it. There will always be areas in which you can grow. God will make those areas evident as you listen to His voice through Scripture, prayer, and the counsel of other believers.

Because you will sometimes fail, you'll need to seek forgiveness from God and others just as you do in your occupation. The person who fails to show up to prepare the sanctuary for a service and the pastor who betrays a church member's confidentiality are both equally responsible for confessing their failures and seeking forgiveness. Forgiveness must be sought from God and from those who were affected by the failure.

Forgiveness should never be something Christian servants frown on. In what other context should Christians be more committed to freely confessing their faults to one another? Sadly, though, Christian service may be the area in which believers feel least willing to confess their failures. Be quick to seek forgiveness when you injure another. If you make a biting remark to a fellow servant, go to that person as soon as you can and ask for forgiveness. If someone comes to you seeking forgiveness, don't brush him off. Rather, warmly offer forgiveness and reconciliation.

Conclusion

Being overworked is a key reason why people leave Christian service. So if you've never become involved in Christian service, you have more to offer than you think. By jumping in, you'll help not only those whom you are serving directly but also your fellow ministers who are probably overworked.

If you have difficulty with saying no, you especially must beware of the peril of becoming overworked. If you overcommit yourself in Christian service, you will cease to have time for the Lord to minister to you. You can serve others only to the degree to which you are served by the Lord in your own spiritual life. If you are always filling an urgent need for Sunday school classes and thereby never attending the service, you may not be letting God sufficiently minister to you. Make it a commitment to let the Lord minister to you as you minister to others.

Conflict also is a common reason why people leave Christian service. The way you relate to fellow servants is as significant as the way you relate to those whom you are serving. For example, if you're on a short-term mission trip rebuilding homes in an area devastated by a natural catastrophe, you might think your main concern is relating well to the locals. But the way you relate to others on your mission team has a major influence on other team members' involvement in future mission trips. It might also give you greater influence on the locals. If they see you exhibiting Christ's love to each other, they will receive a picture of Christian love and community that may be a primary influence in their coming to faith. You are called to love those you serve and also to love those you serve alongside.

Assignment

Read *Session 7: Ministry in the Home*.

Complete the *Life Vision: Action Steps, The Home* exercise beginning on page 121.

Ministry in the Home

In this session, you'll explore having a ministry mindset in your family. This context of ministry is often the most personal and emotional. You may feel deeply connected to your family and motivated to serve them. Or you may feel alienated from your family members and question whether a ministry with them is even possible. Regardless of your situation, you can make it a priority to serve those whom you have come to call family. They may be those who raised you, those whom you have raised or are raising, or those with whom you were raised. Take time in this session to consider how you can be an ambassador and servant of Christ to your family.

Session Aims

Individual Aim: To reevaluate your vision of ministry in the home and identify action steps that will help you attain it.

Group Aim: To encourage and support each other in the process of developing action steps for ministry in the home.

Preparation

Read *Session 7: Ministry in the Home.*

Complete the *Life Vision: Action Steps, The Home* exercise beginning on page 121.

Introduction

No matter your family role—single adult, grandparent, daughter, married parent—you have the responsibility to minister to your family members. The responsibility we have to family members is of highest priority within the command to love others as Christ loved us. The New Testament writers had a lot to say about how family members should relate to one

60

another (see Ephesians 5:22–6:4; Colossians 3:18-21; 1 Timothy 5:4,16; 1 Peter 3:1-7). These passages are full of instructions for husbands, wives, fathers, mothers, siblings, children, and other relatives. How can you fulfill your responsibilities to your family with the attitude of a servant, just as Christ did when He took on the form of a servant (see Philippians 2:5-8)?

Content

In Mark 7, Jesus passionately rebuked a group of Pharisees (Jewish religious leaders) for neglecting the fifth commandment, "Honor your father and your mother" (Exodus 20:12). The fifth commandment is the first one that deals with relations among human beings. Strikingly, it even comes before the commandment against murder. Jesus accused the Pharisees of developing traditions that nullified the responsibility to honor one's parents:

> And he said to them: "You have a fine way of setting aside the commands of God in order to observe your own traditions! For Moses said, 'Honor your father and your mother,' and, 'Anyone who curses his father or mother must be put to death.' But you say that if a man says to his father or mother: 'Whatever help you might otherwise have received from me is Corban' (that is, a gift devoted to God), then you no longer let him do anything for his father or mother. Thus you nullify the word of God by your tradition that you have handed down. And you do many things like that." (Mark 7:9-13)

The Pharisees had created an arrangement whereby they could insulate their assets from the responsibility to care for their elderly parents. It was like refusing today to help pay your needy elderly parent's hospital bills because that would infringe on your 25 percent tithe to the church. Or saying that you can't help out because your money is wrapped up in a retirement fund. While this example of neglect toward family members involves money, there are many examples that don't.

Suppose you live in the same town as your grandson and he plays on a Little League team on Saturdays. What kind of ministry are you going to have in his life if you constantly tell him you can't make it to his games because you play tennis every Saturday afternoon with a friend? You may even rationalize your choice by saying you are a witness to your tennis partner.

If you live at a great distance from family, it may be easy for you to operate with the motto "Out of sight, out of mind." However, telephones and e-mail enable you to be involved with family members from a distance. In addition, the way you use vacation time demonstrates the level of priority you place on family relationships.

The parental role is also crucial. Though we may not often think in terms of serving our kids, parenting is a servant role. As a parent, you serve your children by training them in such a way that they will reap gigantic dividends in the future. You repeatedly rebuke them for offensive speech toward others. You ingrain in them a respect for others, especially for authority figures, such as teachers, coaches, and employers. You encourage them to pursue endeavors (such as music and sports) that will further their growth and development. You take time to enter their world and listen to what's on their minds. You do all that as service to your child. You freely give of yourself for their benefit.

Finally, your marriage relationship is a ministry. Far too often, spouses neglect to ask how they can minister to each other. While couples may discuss their parenting, they rarely ask each other, "What can I do to make you feel appreciated?" or "What do you need and want from me as your partner?" Just as they need God to minister to them so they can serve in the church, parents need their spouses to minister to them so they can serve their children. This is one reason why single parenting is especially difficult.

Don't be like the Pharisees, who created ways to neglect service to their families. Seek wisdom from God on how you can minister to your family.

Conclusion

Family relationships can be stretching. You may feel patronized around your brothers if you are the youngest sibling, even though you are forty-two and have three kids of your own. You may feel disconnected from your sister whom you have seen only twice in ten years. You may be going through a time of tension with your spouse. Or you may struggle with your father's constant disapproval of your majoring in literature instead of premed.

You can always grow in ministry to your family, even though you may find this context of ministry to be the hardest of all. Your style of relating to some family members has been ingrained in you from early childhood.

Those habits are hard to change. But with the Spirit's guidance, strength gained through prayer, and the support of a community of other believers, you can make great strides in this area.

Assignment

Read *Sessions 8–10: Life Vision Presentations*.

Prepare a "Life Vision" presentation by using the guidance of sessions 8–10.

Life Vision Presentations

We have been discussing your ministry vision for various roles and the corresponding action steps. In this session, you will present your own life vision and listen to that of others. These presentations will summarize each person's ministry vision statements and action steps for the group. It will be a great time to encourage and build each other up.

Session Aims

Individual Aim: To present and listen to the "Life Vision" presentations.

Group Aim: To support, counsel, and encourage fellow group members in their ministry visions.

Preparation

Read *Sessions 8–10: Life Vision Presentations*.

With the following guidance, prepare a "Life Vision" presentation.

Introduction

Have you ever known people who were "naturals"? Perhaps they could play the piano without training. Maybe they had great athletic ability without coaching. Or maybe they could paint beautiful pictures without having been taught the fine points of visual art. These people's skills are impressive precisely because they are so unusual. The rest of us have to put in intentional sustained effort in order to acquire such a skill.

For some people ministry comes naturally, but for most of us it requires intentional sustained effort and discipline. If we are to live lives of service, lives "worthy of our calling" (Ephesians 4:1, NET), we must make plans and discipline ourselves to implement them.

Content

Ministry takes discipline simply because it requires an others-centeredness—an "ours for others" attitude that runs counter to the "ours for ourselves" mentality that pervades our culture and often our own hearts. As Christians we are redeemed people, but we are unfinished. The Holy Spirit is transforming our longings and allegiances, but we are still susceptible to the self-centered patterns of the world and the flesh.

Such ingrained patterns can make us view our work as just a means to accumulate wealth, power, or prestige; or conversely, we might see our employer as the one who withholds from us wealth, power, or prestige. We come to view our work in terms of "What can I get from them?" or "What are they keeping from me?" It takes discipline to transform our thinking and practice to reflect a "What can I give?" mentality. *What can I give to my employer so as to honor God? What can I give my coworkers because God has put me here to meet the needs of people He loves?* As we ask and answer these questions and implement concrete action steps, we will minister effectively in our workplaces.

Similarly, we might read a book on the differences between men and women but focus only on finding out what we need from our spouse. It takes discipline to overcome this self-centered tendency and focus on what our spouse needs from us. It takes effort to try to meet those needs, whether our spouse is meeting ours or not. It takes planning and follow-through to minister to a spouse, especially when we don't feel like it.

When we implement concrete action steps, we move from *intuitive* ministry to *intentional* ministry. Intuitive ministry is ministry we find ourselves doing because something within us (the Spirit perhaps?) prompts us to do so. Perhaps you strike up a conversation with a coworker because you feel a burden for him and discover he has a need you can address. Or maybe one of your friends from church comes to mind, so you drop her a note of encouragement and find out later that she really needed it. It's a great feeling to know you have touched someone's life in this way.

However, the problem with intuitive ministry is that it's haphazard and dependent on fluctuating feelings. We can easily miss great opportunities to minister if we aren't struck with just the right feelings at the right times or if we fail to actually act on what we intuitively sense we need to do.

Intentional ministry, on the other hand, doesn't rely on feelings or intuition. It involves careful consideration of how best to minister in a given context. It takes consistent action on behalf of those whom we seek to serve. It involves intentional sustained effort, but it's worth it because it has the power to transform lives.

Intentional ministry involves asking and answering questions such as these:

- Within each context, what are my roles? (See session 3.)
- In each of those roles, what is my level of involvement and what are my responsibilities?
- What are the needs of those to whom I relate in these roles?
- How can I practically and effectively fulfill my responsibilities and meet the identified needs, given the resources God has given me?

Asking and answering such questions helps us develop action steps so we can minister intentionally.

Conclusion

How might it affect a lonely person at work if you made it a discipline to go out of your way just to stick your head in his or her office, smile, and say good morning every day? How might it affect a neighbor whose husband just left her if your family invited her and her kids over for dinner on a regular basis? How might it affect a friend who you know needs Christ if you simply asked him if you could pray for him and then did it? How might it affect your child if you carved out a significant amount of time every week and devoted it only to him? The transformative power of intentional ministry is tremendous. To experience it, we must develop practical action steps, discipline ourselves to carry them out, and ask the Spirit of God to empower our efforts.

Life Vision Presentations

Now you're ready to put together your "Life Vision" presentation. Take the information you accumulated in the "Ministry Vision Statement" exercise and the three "Life Vision: Action Steps" exercises and organize it into a fifteen-minute presentation.

Use whatever approach you like to communicate your vision. You may use props, such as photos of some of the people you will serve. You may hand out lists of your action steps so the group can follow along as you talk. Your presentation need not be elaborate; impressing others isn't the goal. Make sure your presentation takes no more than fifteen minutes.

Assignment

Read *Session 11: For the Glory of Christ*.

Complete *Biblical Exercise: Romans 15* beginning on page 69.

For the Glory of Christ

The short-term goal of this study is to encourage you to see your whole life as a ministry and develop a personal vision for your service to others. The ultimate goal, however, is that Christ be glorified because you are living with a ministry attitude. This concluding session will help you step back and consider the impact of a group of believers living with a ministry mindset.

Session Aims

Individual Aim: To reflect on how your life brings glory to Christ when you live according to your ministry vision.

Group Aim: To consider how much Christ is glorified when an entire Christian community lives with a ministry mindset.

Preparation

Read *Session 11: For the Glory of Christ*.

Complete *Biblical Exercise: Romans 15* beginning on page 69.

Introduction

Consider the following possibility: All of the people in your church have recently begun to see their entire lives as ministry. They're seeing their occupations as places where they can represent Christ. They have reflected on the character traits they need in order to best represent Christ to coworkers and are starting to implement changes. Individuals who previously were only receivers of ministry at church are now serving there as well. Families also are being transformed. Parents, sons, and daughters are ministering to one another.

Can you imagine a community of believers—living like this? How would they affect the broader community? Imagine the influence in a company in which ministry-minded Christians are scattered throughout the organization, from the top leadership down to the lowest-paying position. Imagine what church events and programs would be like. When a visitor came to a church event, what would he observe? Imagine the impact in a community if all the families in your church body had a ministry mindset. What would be the effect on neighborhood gatherings, Little League games, and birthday parties?

Content

The point here is not that your culture can become entirely Christian, a paradise on earth. Rather, the point is to consider the impact Christians can have. All too often, believers leave their faith locked away in some private part of their heart. This approach is inconsistent with the Christian faith. Christ calls us not only to forgiveness from sin and acceptance by God but also to repentance, transformation, and active love for others. His call involves adopting the attitude of a servant (see Philippians 2:3-11).

Christ's servant attitude and behavior led to His exaltation. Because we have become identified with Christ, we too are called to take on a servant attitude that leads to Christ's exaltation. If our Christian communities reflect this attitude, our neighbors will take notice and some will be drawn to enter the community of faith.

At the heart of a ministry mindset is love. Our calling is most fundamentally a calling to love. We are called to experience our Father's love and then exercise love for others:

> I pray that out of his glorious riches he may strengthen you with power through his Spirit in your inner being, so that Christ may dwell in your hearts through faith. And I pray that you, being rooted and established in love, may have power, together with all the saints, to grasp how wide and long and high and deep is the love of Christ, and to know this love that surpasses knowledge—that you may be filled to the measure of all the fullness of God. (Ephesians 3:16-19)

This is love: not that we loved God, but that he loved us and sent his Son as an atoning sacrifice for our sins. Dear friends, since God so loved us, we also ought to love one another. (1 John 4:10-11)

While our ministry of love (others-orientation, sacrifice, honesty) in the world might lead to the conversion of unbelievers, their conversion is not our responsibility. God is the One who draws persons into relationship with Himself. When people are reconciled to Him and when believers' lives are transformed by His love, God is glorified. He is the agent of reconciliation and transformation. Yet He is exalted when His children cooperate with Him in His work.

Conclusion

Not only is ministry part of our calling but it also leads to the most fulfilling life we can have. May you experience the fullness of Christ's love, and may your experience of that love overflow in service to others. Johann Sebastian Bach signed all of his compositions *Soli Deo Gloria*, which means "to God only be glory." May all that we do be signed with those words.

Biblical Exercise: Romans 15

Read Romans 15:1-13. Also, review "A Method for the Biblical Exercises" beginning on page 17.

Observation — **"What Do I See?"**

1. Who are the persons (including God) in the passage? What is the condition of those persons?

2. What subjects did Paul discuss in the passage? What did he assert?

3. Note the sequence in which Paul made these assertions. (You might number them in order.)

4. What did Paul emphasize? Are there repeated ideas and themes? How are the various parts related?

5. Why did Paul write this passage? (Did he say anything about ways he expected the reader to change after reading it?)

Interpretation Phase 1 — "What Did It Mean Then?"

1. Coming to Terms—Are there any words in the passage that you don't understand? Write down anything you found confusing about the passage.

2. Finding Where It Fits—What clues does the Bible give about the meaning of this passage?

   • Immediate Context (the passage being studied)

   • Remote Context (passages that come before and after the one being studied)

3. Getting into Their Sandals—An Exercise in Imagination

   • What are the main points of this passage? Summarize or write an outline of the passage.

- What do you think the recipients of the letter were supposed to take from this passage? How did God, inspiring Paul to write Romans, want this passage to impact the Roman believers?

Interpretation Phase 2 — **"What Does It Mean Now?"**

1. What is the timeless truth in the passage? In one or two sentences, write down what you learned about God from Romans 15.

2. How does that truth work today?

Application — **"What Can I Do to Make This Truth Real?"**

1. What can I do to make this truth real for myself?

2. For my family?

3. For my friends?

4. For the people who live near me?

5. For the rest of the world?

Life Vision

Introduction

"Life Vision" is a tool to help you assess all of the resources God has given you—spiritual gifts, character, abilities, interests, formative experiences, and material possessions—so you can evaluate how you can minister to others' needs. This tool will guide you in developing a ministry vision in every area of your life—in the world, in the church, and in the home.

In each of those areas, you have particular roles. A role is a specific position or set of responsibilities a person holds. For example, in the world you may be both an engineer and a chairperson for your Neighborhood Watch Association, while in the church you are a Sunday school teacher and a missions committee member. This tool will help you identify a vision for ministry in your various roles.

The "Life Vision" tool begins by taking inventory of all the resources you have been given. Then it leads you through a process of evaluating your various roles and the needs of others around you in each role. You'll develop a ministry vision for several of your main roles. Your vision statements will help you focus on styles of relating that meet needs you have the resources to meet. Finally, this tool will help you set action steps for each ministry vision statement.

You'll do the "Life Vision" exercises in private. Each exercise provides instructions. To illustrate the type of response expected for each exercise, there are sample completed worksheets written from the perspective of a fictional character. The same fictional character will be used in each exercise so you can see continuity from one exercise to the next.

In addition, there are several spiritual discipline exercises scattered throughout. These give you a chance to exercise a spiritual discipline that relates to the corresponding "Life Vision" exercise.

You'll get out of the exercises what you put into them in terms of the amount of time and attention invested. This process can be a significant time for you to increase your understanding of your ministry as an ambassador for Christ.

Though "Life Vision" may be used profitably by individuals, it has been designed for small-group interaction. Sharing with the group will help solidify your vision for ministry in each area of your life. Also, group members can provide accountability for one another to follow through on the action steps and help each other reevaluate ministry vision in the future.

Personal Inventory, Part I

In parts I and II of "Personal Inventory," you will assess who you are in order to see the resources you have to serve others. In part I, you'll record observations about your spiritual gifts and character. In part II, you'll note your abilities, interests, formative experiences, and material possessions. In some categories, you may have a great deal to record. In others, you may have little to record. We have provided examples to help you understand what is meant by each category.

Be honest about yourself. There is no pressure to come up with talents or skills that seem impressive. On the other hand, don't fail to record aspects of yourself that seem too secular or irrelevant to ministry.

Spiritual Gifts

Spiritual gifts are personal resources that God has entrusted to you. They are used mainly in the church or among another group of believers rather than among unbelievers. While there is much debate regarding lists of spiritual gifts, the following list includes gifts that are broadly accepted:
- Exhortation
- Service
- Teaching
- Encouragement
- Giving
- Leadership
- Mercy
- Administration

To begin the process of identifying your spiritual gifts, reflect on Romans 12:1-8 and 1 Corinthians 12:1-31. Assess what gifts you have in light of the Scripture reading, counsel with other believers, and past experience. The questions on pages 78-79 will help you do this.

If you have limited experience in ministry, you may not have much to write in response to the questions. If you are unable to give any response to certain questions, keep them in the back of your mind to consider after you have gained some firsthand experience in ministry. If you are completely unclear about your spiritual gifts, you may skip this section and go on to the "Interests" section. Later, when you have more experience in ministry, you may find it helpful to come back to this section. If you have any questions about what spiritual gifts are or what a particular gift is, ask your small-group leader or pastor.

1. What aspects of ministry do I enjoy doing? (For example, leading a third-grade Sunday school class, participating in an evangelistic outreach program, giving practical help to small-group members who need help.)

2. What aspects of ministry do others enjoy or benefit from when I am doing them?

3. What aspects of ministry have I been affirmed in by others in the community?

4. When I look at the church today, what do I see as the church's greatest need?

Record your spiritual gifts on page 80. Indicate not merely your areas of giftedness but also how you most enjoy exercising your gifts. Here are some examples:

- Teaching: I enjoy teaching lessons to third-graders and seeing them learn biblical narratives and principles.
- Administration: I have enjoyed doing administrative work at the Pregnancy Center at my church.
- Service: I like preparing the sanctuary for worship on Sunday mornings.
- Mercy: When someone I know is in the hospital, I like to visit the person or provide meals for his or her family.
- Encouragement: I'm the person people call when they need someone to listen to a problem and care for them without being too quick with advice.
- Giving: I am fulfilled when I can help financially with special needs of youth ministries in our city.

My Spiritual Gifts

Character

Understanding the issues that help you live by your convictions or hinder you from doing so can guide you in choosing how you'll live as a minister of Christ daily. Character strengths and weaknesses, along with personality issues, are important to bear in mind as you think about what you have to offer through service to others.

On page 81, describe the key aspects of your character. Record your past character weaknesses. For instance, maybe you've struggled with lying at your workplace or home, or perhaps you've had a poor work ethic in a position that gave great flexibility in your schedule. Also, record your character strengths. You may have had success honestly communicating your concerns with your boss while refraining from gossiping about her to coworkers. Or you may have remained committed to fulfilling your responsibilities as a parent in spite of opportunities to move up the company ladder by working longer hours.

Finally, record issues that relate to your personality, including those that affect how you tend to relate to others and do your work. For example, perhaps you like to work on tasks as a team rather than alone. Or perhaps you tend to seek resolution to conflict or tend to ignore conflict. These are not necessarily character strengths or weaknesses but rather personality traits. The following are examples of character:

- I ask questions in order to hear others, understand their needs, and serve them in appropriate ways.
- I stay committed to revealing my intentions, desires, feelings of deficiency, and personal failures to my spouse and a few close friends.
- I'm most motivated when I work with others.
- I avoid having a public or private meal alone with a member of the opposite sex.
- I limit extra commitments to the extent that I can be readily available to my spouse and kids.
- I take my complaints directly to a person rather than speaking about them to others.
- I increasingly avoid my tendency to think that my solution is always the best solution.
- I realize that what seems most productive and effective is not always what is best according to ethical principles.
- I restrain myself from becoming angry too quickly.
- I make time in my schedule to gain a biblical perspective on life and ministry.
- I focus on a few priorities that I can do excellently rather than on too many priorities that I can't fulfill well.

My Character

Personal Inventory, Part II

You will continue with your personal inventory by recording observations about your abilities, interests, formative experiences, and material possessions. These are additional resources out of which you can serve others. Take your time recording as much as you can in each area. Even qualities that may seem irrelevant to ministry can be offered in service to others.

Abilities and Interests

Your abilities include both natural talents and learned skills. Record things you do well, whether you do them in your occupation, at church, or around the house. An ability may be a natural propensity to make people feel at ease or to make them laugh. Or you may be able to coordinate events effectively. Maybe you can type ninety words per minute. You may have developed the expertise to manage finances. Whatever your abilities are, even if you think they are trivial or irrelevant, record them on page 85. We have provided some examples, but there are many talents and skills not listed here that may apply to you. The following examples might help you identify your abilities:

- Analyze a large amount of data and provide a useful summary
- Make a space beautiful or comfortable
- Coordinate people and resources for events
- Create something artistic
- Revise and edit written documents
- Pack and store items in an organized and efficient manner
- Make people feel welcome and comfortable
- Act in dramatic productions
- Make wise decisions in the midst of great complexity
- Motivate or encourage others to start something new or stay committed
- Perform a trade (carpentry, landscaping, electrical, farming)
- Teach children or adults through a curriculum
- Manage financial resources
- Perform musically (vocal or instrumental)
- Probe or analyze in order to address quality control or integrity

- Manage and follow through with details (office administration or household management)
- Think of innovative solutions to problems

Consider your past experiences and current circumstances to also identify your interests. Record your valued interests on page 85 as well. As with your abilities, these areas may seem irrelevant to ministry. Record them anyway. They may include an interest in car maintenance and repair, fashion, sports, investments, community service, or collections (such as coins or art).

Your interests may or may not be related to your occupation. For instance, you may be an electrical engineer yet have great interest in the stock market, or you may be a nurse and be interested in video production. Also, your interests may be areas that have a direct relationship to ministry, or they may not seem related at all. This list of interests might help you come up with your own:
- Learning and using new technology
- Leading small-group discussions
- Managing finances or resources
- Experiencing cultural diversity
- Helping those who are poor and homeless
- Equipping believers to be effective witnesses in their workplaces
- Playing and coaching sports
- Enabling foreigners to adjust to American culture
- Helping with musical or dramatic performances
- Providing manual labor for setup or cleanup for events
- Camping and experiencing outdoor activities

Abilities and Interests — sample

- Fishing: I started fishing as a kid and continue my love of fishing with my wife. We fish several times a year at local lakes.
- Implementation and problem solving: I can efficiently figure out ways to reach a given objective. At work, whenever there's a change in our line of products or our procedures, I can figure out how to overcome obstacles and make things run smoothly.
- Budgeting: I'm good at working with our home finances, determining how we can make wise investments with our savings, and keeping our spending within good limits.

- Baseball: I have a share in four season tickets with a friend. My wife and I like to go with several other couples and do tailgate parties before or after the games.
- Technology: I have always been good at working with technology, whether it's repairing appliances around the house or building computers from parts. I can learn how to use new technology quickly.
- Landscaping and lawn maintenance: I have come to enjoy the manual labor involved in and sense of accomplishment gained from working in my yard. I have redesigned our landscaping with plants and flower beds. It gives me a chance to be outside after working in an office all day.
- Cookouts: If we aren't at a ball game on summer weekends, we love to invite friends over to our place for a barbecue. We sit on our back porch and enjoy the conversation and good food.

My Abilities and Interests

Formative Experiences

Next you will record some of your most significant experiences that have shaped you into the person you are. These past experiences are a fundamental part of you and can be resources from which to serve others. Formative experiences include significant relationships and life-changing events or time periods. The following are examples of formative experiences:

- Spending every afternoon of my elementary school years with my grandmother, a godly Christian woman who struggled with chronic pain, increased my desire to encourage and support those who live with pain and illness.
- Failing to make the basketball team as a junior in high school led me to develop my interest in music.
- My parents' divorce when I was in college has marked me with anxiety about marriage in my future.
- A learning disability has made me struggle with my confidence and ability to contribute whenever I'm in a new environment.

My Formative Experiences

Material Possessions

Jesus often addressed the issue of money and possessions. For example, in Luke 18:18-30 we read about an interaction between Jesus and a rich man, with the discussion revolving around the man's wealth. Private property is of great importance in Western culture. The question for us is whether or not we hold our possessions and money loosely and let God use them in service to others.

Make a record of your material resources. Don't worry about the monetary value of your possessions, but think about how you can use things such as your home, vehicles, finances, food, land, or other material possessions to serve others. Here are some examples:

- Two spare bedrooms in our home
- A small fishing boat
- An old Chevy Suburban (used for tailgate parties and fishing trips)
- An old desktop computer
- A large back porch and yard ideal for parties and gatherings
- Half ownership of baseball season tickets
- Deluxe, oversized barbecue grill

My Material Possessions

Spiritual Discipline Exercise — Hospitality

One of the disciplines widely recognized in the Christian tradition is the discipline of hospitality. "Personal Inventory" provides an ideal opportunity to ask yourself, *How can I give of myself to others?* Consider intentionally hosting some people to enjoy a meal at your house, in your backyard, at a park, or at a restaurant. Treat a person or group of people to a casual, refreshing time. Maybe God will bring someone across your path this week whom you can invite—an old friend, a new acquaintance, or a former coworker. Or this may be the time to invite someone with whom you have wanted to get together. Write down your plan for hosting and whom you will invite.

Roles and Needs

In this exercise, you will identify the roles you hold in the three primary contexts of ministry. Roles include being an employee, a husband or wife, a father or mother, a church member, a citizen, or a participant on a team. In the first column on pages 91, 93, and 95, list all of your roles. Then in the second column, write down the needs you observe in that role. The following questions may be helpful as you think through the needs in each role:

- What issues do other people commonly complain about in that role? ("There's never enough water on this job site," "I can never find the forms I'm looking for," "This closet is totally disorganized.")
- What important tasks are always neglected? ("The trash cans never get emptied," "The details of the project are never adequately addressed," "The instructions are never adequately communicated.")
- How do people need to be treated? ("Nobody helps me when I have questions," "New employees are rarely introduced to the group," "Nobody ever asks me how I'm doing.")

Ask others for their thoughts about needs in your various roles. For example, you may ask your spouse what needs she thinks your kids have, given their personalities. Or you may ask a fellow believer in a similar industry about the needs in his workplace. You may call another member of the group to ask her opinion. In these ways, you may discover needs in your own roles that you haven't considered before. Please review the following sample charts before filling in your personal information.

In the World — sample

Roles	Needs
Accountant	People work on their own projects and there is no sense of teamwork with tasks. Therefore, there is constant pressure to meet deadlines.
Neighbor	I live in a town house with attached garage and rarely see my neighbors. Everyone would like to have a greater sense of connection between neighbors.
Customer Service Consultant	Trust and respect between the twenty service consultants, including my level of trust and respect for other consultants. Because we all handle cases individually for customers, we don't tend to get to know each other. Also, there's a lot of competition among the consultants. I think everyone could lighten up to some degree.
Basketball League	I play basketball with a group of guys in a league, but the league keeps increasing fees such that some guys can no longer afford the cost.
Baseball Tailgate Organizer	Although it's not a formal role, I'm the organizer of tailgate parties among our group of friends. Our friends are starting to have kids and our spot for tailgating isn't suited for kids, so some of our friends with children have stopped coming.

In the World

Roles	Needs

In the Church — sample

Roles	Needs
Regular Church Attender	I think visitors need to be more warmly greeted. When the service ends, not many people stay to chat with each other. Most attenders just head to their cars right away.
Parking Attendant	Because we have a shortage of parking spots, people can get frustrated and angry about finding parking.
Giver of Money	I have a hard time knowing if I should include my giving to missionary friends in my official 10 percent tithe or if I should think of it as separate giving.
Accountability Partner	A friend and I meet over breakfast to be accountable to each other for our integrity and spiritual growth. Unfortunately, it's become routine. We ask each other the same few questions every time, and our answers are always "safe."
Social Committee	Everything has been run the same way for years without any changes or new ideas. The traditional church events have not been evaluated for improvement.

In the Church

Roles	Needs

In the Home — sample

Roles	Needs
Husband	I'm learning a lot about my wife at this early stage of our marriage. She needs me to listen to her and try to understand how she feels. She expects us to do lots of little, everyday tasks (fixing dinner, cleaning up, working on the house, discussing budget issues) together.
Son	My parents have recently been struggling with having an empty nest. Both my brother and I have moved away, and my parents have realized they don't have many friends. They poured so much of their lives and energy into us that they're now wondering what to do with themselves.
Wife	My husband never made any close guy friends since we moved several years ago. He doesn't seem to have an outlet for talking to other men about issues of being a husband and father. He also doesn't have friends with whom to do activities that he loves.
Father	My thirteen-year-old son is beginning to need more independence and opportunity to make his own decisions.
Daughter	My elderly father is at the point of needing more help (shopping, cooking, cleaning). He is now unable to drive and has trouble remembering important things such as taking his medication and paying bills.

In the Home

Roles	Needs

Ministry Vision Statement

This exercise is both the hardest one to complete and the most important. You will write a personal vision statement for your most significant roles. These vision statements will paint a picture of what you want your ministry to look like in those roles.

You will work with one role at a time and review the needs you identified in that role. Your first step will be to compare the needs you identified in the "Roles and Needs" exercise with the resources you identified in the "Personal Inventory, Part I" exercise. Try to match the needs with your resources. This process can be put in the following terms:

> I will minister as a [your role] by meeting the need(s) of _____
> with my resource(s) of _____.

Some people find this step of matching needs and resources to be motivating. They find it helps them develop a vision statement. Other people are more intuitive. They prefer to come up with a ministry vision without deliberately thinking through their resources and the needs. Instead, they may approach their ministry vision by answering the question "What will I want other employees to say of me when I move on?" or "What will I want my kids to say of me as a father?"

Both approaches are helpful. Even if you take the more intuitive approach, it is imperative that you go back and think about how your vision meets needs in that particular role and confirm that you have the necessary personal resources to offer. Both approaches—the more broad-strokes, intuitive approach and the more methodical approach of matching needs with resources—will help you come up with a good vision statement. If you initially take the methodical approach, you should also think about what that will look like in the end. Will that vision be compelling to those you hope to serve? Will it contribute to spreading the knowledge of God and building up others?

For examples of developing ministry vision statements, read the following four case studies. The first two case studies use the context of ministry in the world. (Thinking about ministry in the world is often harder than thinking about ministry in the home or church because you are often restricted from serving explicitly as a representative of Christ. This will be evident in the first two case studies.) The third and fourth case studies will involve ministry in the church and in the home, respectively.

Bruce the Basketball Coach

Bruce is a high school basketball coach who notices that many of his players have no father figure or male role model. He tries to spend time with them himself, but he can do only so much because he also teaches and is married with three kids at home. Bruce's experience with the Big Brother and Big Sister mentoring programs as a college student makes him think that his players need some sort of mentoring. Bruce considers the possibility of establishing a mentoring program for his players.

Through his relationships with members of the athletic booster club and his involvement in the community for the last eight years, he knows plenty of respected men in town who could be mentors. He has administrative skills and extra time in the summer to organize the process of connecting student-athletes with respected adults in the community. Bruce puts together a vision by matching his resources with an identified need. He comes up with the following vision statement:

"I will serve as a high school basketball coach by meeting the need for male role models in my players' lives by establishing a mentoring program of respected men in the community. Whenever the opportunity arises, I will share with others that my motivation to serve my players in this way comes from my relationship with Christ."

Notice that Bruce's vision for ministry in this case study adds an entirely new dimension to his role as a coach. This will not be true for each ministry vision (see the case of "Kim the Corporate Cubical Worker" below). Also, notice that there is nothing explicitly Christian about his mentoring program, because he works at a public school. Rather, the Christian element of his vision is in his own motivation to be a witness by the manner in which he is a basketball coach. He hopes the way he fulfills his role will lead to many opportunities for him to share about his faith with his players, their parents, and members of the community.

The overarching command for every believer is to love God and love others (see Matthew 22:37-40). The question each of us must answer is "How?" Bruce has already committed himself to loving his players as their coach. The issue is how he can do so to the best of his ability with all of his available resources.

In addition, notice that Bruce's vision statement doesn't address how to implement his vision. In his action steps, which he will develop after he solidifies his vision, he will address the following questions: *How will I communicate this program to the athletic director? What do I need to do to get permission to start the program? How will I communicate the program to my players? What will be the standards for determining whether or not someone is a "respected member of the community"? What will be the guidelines for their mentoring relationship (where they should meet, what they should discuss, and so on)?* The answers to these questions will be the action steps. You will deal with action steps later.

Kim the Corporate Cubical Worker

Kim has been working at the I.M.A. corporate headquarters for four years. She has noticed that new employees who are single struggle to settle in to both the company and the community. Because the company is located in a family-oriented suburb, many employees happen to be married with children. While Kim has learned how to enjoy leading a single life in the company and the community, she has observed many singles who have left before discovering the opportunities and activities that she found over time.

Kim is committed to having an excellent work ethic and integrity in her relationships with coworkers. However, she feels she can serve new single employees informally by taking the initiative to invite them to join her and her friends in many of their activities and social events (dinner parties, church singles gatherings, concerts at the park). Kim's inclination to find out about such opportunities and her past experience in the community give her the resources to serve in this way. She is also highly extraverted and makes people feel at ease and welcomed. She has developed good friendships with men and women so that she can invite both to gatherings without either feeling uncomfortable. Kim's vision statement is:

"I will intentionally serve new single employees at I.M.A. by helping them adjust to the community. While I hope to serve their felt needs for experiencing a sense of community, I hope that I, my friends, or exposure to any church activities they may attend also will cause them to be drawn to faith in Christ."

Kim's ministry vision does not require her to add any new component to her life. She is merely trying to develop a ministry vision within the normal aspects of her life in the world. Her vision simply adds a level of intentionality and initiative with others, yet this added initiative can have significant impact on those new employees.

Ted the Church Attender

Ted has been attending Grace Church for three years. He went through the membership class and consistently gives money to the church. He realizes, though, that he hasn't once served anyone else in the church with his time and energy. Ted hears an announcement at a service that volunteers are needed to help with the church's caregiving ministry. This announcement makes an impression on Ted because he helped care for his uncle for several years until his uncle passed away last spring. Ted's uncle lived close by, so Ted visited him several times a week and dropped off any groceries or medications his uncle needed. His patience with his uncle surprised even Ted.

Although Ted doesn't know his spiritual gifts, he calls the church and asks to talk to someone with the caregiving ministry. Within a week, he joins another church member on visits to some of the elderly in the church, helping out in any way needed. Ted decides that his ministry vision statement is:

"I will serve in whatever capacity is needed for the caregiving ministry at Grace Church with an attitude of learning. I hope my service will encourage others who share in the ministry and that my service with the elderly will lead them to belief in Christ or growth in their faith."

Ted's example comes from the church context. Notice that Ted is convicted to take on a new ministry role at his church. You may realize there is a ministry role you should be involved in but are not. Take time to ask God if He wants you to be involved in a new ministry role.

Also, notice that Ted's vision statement is simple and unrefined; he merely wants to jump in and help out in any way. Later Ted may refine his vision statement to focus on a specific area of service within the caregiving ministry. Perhaps he will identify that his most significant area of service is in administration or in facilitating a caregivers' support group. But for now, a general vision is fine.

Judy the Aunt

Judy and her husband of fifteen years have been unable to have children. Judy's sister, however, lives nearby and has two boys and two girls. Judy's nephews are ages eight and twelve, and her nieces are ages ten and fifteen. While Judy has seen the kids during family get-togethers at Christmas, Thanksgiving, Easter, and the Fourth of July, she has never spent much time with them outside of those large gatherings. Judy decides she wants to develop a ministry vision for her relationship with her nieces and nephews.

Because Judy and her husband have an extensive social life, she realizes she will have to be willing to sacrifice some of her normal commitments. But one of the reasons she feels committed to her new vision is that she has long wished that she'd had an adult Christian mentor when she was a teenager. Her nieces and nephews, she notices, don't have any adult mentors.

While she has had no experience mentoring teenagers, at work she has developed into a manager known for her ability to provide wise counsel and support for new trainees. She hopes she can learn to mentor her nieces and nephews in the same way. Her new ministry vision for her relationship with them is:

"I am committed to engaging individually with each of my nieces and nephews in order to demonstrate my love and be available to mentor them. In spite of my lack of involvement in their lives in the past, I hope that through consistent commitment to them and my testimony to Christ's work in my life, they will be drawn to a relationship with Him."

Judy's case study is an example that isn't typical for ministry in the home. Hers is a ministry to family members who don't live with her but are nonetheless part of her family. The typical example for ministry in the home will be as a father or mother, husband or wife, brother or sister, or son or daughter. We offer this case study as an example for those who may not think they have much to offer in the way of ministry to family members.

Now that you have read through the case studies, begin to formulate your own vision statements. Start by identifying the one or two primary roles in each of your contexts, or settings—the world, the church, and the home. You have two charts for each context, although you may use just one if you have only one primary role in that context. (For example, maybe your only significant role in the world is your job.)

For each context (world, church, home), review the sample chart. Then, in the two empty charts, record the name of the role, needs in that role, resources to meet the needs, and a ministry vision statement. You will have a chance to revise your vision statements in an upcoming session, so don't feel this is your only chance. Just focus on making a good first attempt at vision statements.

It's also helpful to realize you are learning a process as much as you are establishing vision statements. Throughout your life, you ought to periodi-cally revisit your vision statements (for instance, when you change jobs) to determine if your vision needs to be adjusted. In this way, you will learn and grow in your ministry to others throughout your life.

How do you want to fulfill your roles in the world? Remember always to pur-sue God's glory above all else. As you seek to glorify God, celebrate the fact that He has given you unique abilities to do so. He has uniquely crafted you in preparation for your service to Him and His people (see Ephesians 2:10).

In the World — sample   Role: *Customer Service Consultant*

Needs	Resources
More trust and respect among coworkers	Backyard and porch for parties
	Skill in grilling and cooking for groups
More friendliness and less competitive attitude	Ability to solve problems and implement plans
	Baseball tailgating
	Spiritual gifts of serving and giving

Ministry Vision:

My vision is to provide opportunities for coworkers to gather in informal settings so that we can get to know each other better and increase our trust, respect, and friendliness. I hope that by offering my resources to increase interaction among coworkers, my relationships will deepen and I will have more opportunities to share my faith.

In the World   **Role:** _____

    Needs   **Resources**

Ministry Vision:

In the World

Role: _____

Needs

Resources

Ministry Vision:

In the Church — sample   Role: *Accountability Partner*

Needs

Make our meetings more
effective and motivating

Spend more time together
outside our accountability
meetings

Resources

Fishing trips

Baseball tailgating

Lawn care and landscaping

Competency in technology

Spiritual gifts of serving and
giving

Ministry Vision:

I want to improve my relationship with my accountability partner by sharing more of our lives with each other. I hope that by doing more activities
together, we will be more effective at understanding how to help each
other in our spiritual growth in Christ.

In the Church   **Role:** _____

      Needs   **Resources**

Ministry Vision:

In the Church   **Role:** _____

      Needs   **Resources**

Ministry Vision:

In the Home — sample   **Role: *Husband***

Needs	Resources
Better listening	Strong work ethic; disciplined to follow through on commitments
Expectations to do more tasks together around the house	Commitment to be home every evening
	Spiritual gift of service
	Problem-solving ability

Ministry Vision:

I am committed to learning to love my wife better by engaging with her in a focused way in our home life. I hope this vision will encourage and honor her in a manner similar to the way Christ loves me.

In the Home

Role: _____

Needs	Resources

Ministry Vision:

In the Home   Role: _____

     Needs   **Resources**

Ministry Vision:

Spiritual Discipline Exercise — Scripture Memory

For each ministry vision statement, find several Bible verses that directly relate to it. If you have trouble finding verses, ask for help from a friend, a family member, or your pastor.

Write the verses on an index card and keep it in your pocket every day of this week. Put the verses in your car or on your bathroom mirror. Commit the verses to memory. When you are getting ready for the day, driving around doing errands, or taking a coffee break, recite the verses. Contemplate how they affect your vision for ministry.

Action Steps,
The World

In this exercise, you will identify tangible action steps for ministry in the world. However, before you work on action steps, you will:

1. Edit or revise your ministry vision statements.

2. Identify obstacles to overcome and sacrifices to make in order to attain your vision.

Take time to revisit your vision statements for ministry in the world. Revise or edit the statements in light of any feedback you received from others or new insights you have gained. Write your vision statements in the appropriate areas on pages 115-116.

Next identify any obstacles to attaining your vision. Record external dynamics that might keep you from attaining your vision. Add sacrifices you will have to make to attain your vision. Personal sacrifices are often what most hinder us from attaining our vision. If you are unwilling to make the necessary sacrifices, you need to reexamine your heart to determine whether you are truly committed to your ministry vision.

Finally, determine steps you can take to overcome obstacles and reach your vision. Make sure they are concrete actions by which you can evaluate yourself. The action steps will guide you toward realizing your ministry vision.

In the World — sample   **Role:** *Customer Service Consultant*

Ministry Vision Statement

My vision is to provide opportunities for coworkers to gather in informal settings so that we can get to know each other better and increase our trust, respect, and friendliness. I hope that by offering my resources to increase interaction among coworkers, my relationships will deepen and I will have more opportunities to share my faith.

Obstacles and Sacrifices

- Competitive attitudes.
- Ongoing pressure of corporate culture to produce individually rather than as teams.
- People's distrust of me.
- I need to choose to be committed to occasionally hosting parties with coworkers rather than always having parties with close friends from outside the office.

Action Steps

- Determine a date for a cookout party for coworkers at my home.
- Determine a date for a baseball tailgate party for coworkers, and find a location that is kid-friendly for those with children.
- Plan food, drinks, and activities that will be attractive to coworkers.
- Put together an invitation list and send out invitations for the events.
- As the date approaches for a gathering, begin to ask coworkers if they will be able to come and encourage them to do so.
- Arrange for all the food and drinks.
- Encourage coworkers to bring their families, friends, or dates so I can meet the important people in their lives.
- Pray that many coworkers respond.

In the World   **Role:** _____

Ministry Vision Statement

Obstacles and Sacrifices

Action Steps

In the World   **Role:** _____

Ministry Vision Statement

Obstacles and Sacrifices

Action Steps

Action Steps, The Church

Repeat the exercise you completed in "Action Steps, The World" but this time think about ministry in the church.

1. Edit or revise your ministry vision statements for the church.

2. Identify obstacles and sacrifices.

3. Record action steps.

In the Church — sample   **Role:** *Accountability Partner*

Ministry Vision Statement

I want to improve my relationship with my accountability partner by sharing more of our lives with each other. I hope that by doing more activities together, we will be more effective at understanding how to help each other in our spiritual growth in Christ.

Obstacles and Sacrifices

- Busy schedules: Because he has a busy home life with a couple of kids, it's hard to find times and activities we can do together.
- Committing to spending time with him: I need to make him a priority by carving time out of my schedule.
- Different stages of life: I'm married without kids, whereas he's married with two kids.

Action Steps

- Invite him and his family to go on a fishing trip with us.
- Offer to help him with his yard work and landscaping because he has mentioned his frustration with keeping his yard up.
- Invite him and his family to our regular tailgate parties and introduce him to our other friends.
- Help him figure out how he can improve his efficiency in his contractor business with new technology, such as computers and daily organizers.
- Find a book he and I can both read to find ways to address issues in each other's lives in a more motivating way.

In the Church **Role:** _____

Ministry Vision Statement

Obstacles and Sacrifices

Action Steps

120

In the Church   **Role:** _____

Ministry Vision Statement

Obstacles and Sacrifices

Action Steps

Action Steps,
The Home

Repeat the exercise you completed in "Action Steps, The Church" but this time, think about ministry in the home.

1. Edit or revise your ministry vision statements for the home.

2. Identify obstacles and sacrifices.

3. Record action steps.

In the Home — sample   **Role:** *Husband*

Ministry Vision Statement

I am committed to learning to love my wife better by engaging with her in a focused way in our home life. I hope this vision will encourage and honor her in a manner similar to the way Christ loves me.

Obstacles and Sacrifices

- My difficulty at listening when there is great emotion.
- Immediately seeking a solution to her problem rather than engaging with her feelings.
- My preference to work on tasks by myself.
- My preference to do tasks by my own standards, not someone else's standards.

Action Steps

- Ask how I can help her, and then be willing to learn the way she wants me to help instead of insisting on my way.
- Turn off the television and put away reading material when in conversation with her.
- Join with her when she is working on a task, such as cleaning up or cooking dinner.
- Every evening, ask how her day was and engage with her in the response she gives.
- Put aside anything I'm working on whenever she asks for my help.

In the Home   **Role:** _____

Ministry Vision Statement

Obstacles and Sacrifices

Action Steps

In the Home   **Role:** _____

Ministry Vision Statement

Obstacles and Sacrifices

Action Steps

Spiritual Discipline Exercise — Accountability

You need accountability from others as you begin to execute your plans for ministry. If you are in a small group doing these exercises, you have a great opportunity to ask for accountability from group members. Commit to remaining in a relationship of accountability with them about your action steps.

Otherwise, seek some accountability from either friends or family so that you can be supported in your plans for ministry. Clarify what exactly you want to be held accountable for, and then ask others to support you.

Leader's Guide

Introduction

This leader's guide will:
- Explain the intended purpose of each session and how each session fits into the entire study
- Provide you with plenty of discussion questions so that you can choose a few that suit your group
- Suggest other ways of interacting over the material

The first step in leading this study is to read "A Model of Spiritual Transformation" beginning on page 9. The section describes three broad approaches to growth and explains how the four studies in the series fit together.

There's more involved in leading a small group, however, than just understanding the study and its objective. The main skill you'll need is creating a group environment that facilitates authentic interaction among people. Every leader does this in his or her own style, but here are two principles necessary for all:

1. *Avoid the temptation to speak whenever people don't immediately respond to one of your questions.* As the leader, you may feel pressure to break the silence. Often, though, leaders overestimate how much silence has gone by. Several seconds of silence may seem like a minute to the leader. However, usually people just need time to collect their thoughts before they respond. If you wait patiently for their responses, they will usually take that to mean you really do want them to say what they think. On the other hand, if you consistently break the silence yourself, they may not feel the need to speak up.

2. *Avoid being a problem solver.* If you immediately try to solve every problem that group members voice, they won't feel comfortable sharing issues of personal struggle. Why? Because most people, when sharing their problems, initially want to receive acceptance

and empathy rather than advice. They want others to understand and care about the troubled state of their soul. Giving immediate advice can often communicate that you feel they are not bright enough to figure out the solution.

Getting a Small Group Started

You may be gathering a group of friends to do a study together or possibly you've volunteered to lead a group that your church is assembling. Regardless of the circumstances, God has identified you as the leader.

You are probably a peer of the other group members. Some may have read more theology than you, some may have more church ministry experience than you, and yet God has providentially chosen you as the leader. You're not the "teacher" or the sole possessor of wisdom—you are simply responsible to create an atmosphere that facilitates genuine interaction.

One of the most effective ways you can serve your group is to *make clear what is expected.* You are the person who informs group members. They need to know, for example, where and when your first meeting will be held. If you're meeting in a home and members need maps, make sure they receive them in a timely manner. If members don't have study books, help them each obtain one. To create a hospitable setting for your meetings, you will need to plan for refreshments or delegate that responsibility to others. A group phone and e-mail list may also be helpful; ask the group if it's okay to distribute their contact information to one another. Make sure there's a sense of order. You may even want to chart out a tentative schedule of all the sessions, including any off weeks for holidays.

The first several sessions are particularly important because they are when you will communicate your vision for the group. You'll want to explain your vision several times during your first several meetings. Many people need to hear it several times before it really sinks in, and some will probably miss the first meeting or two. Communicate your vision and expectations concisely so that plenty of time remains for group discussion. People will drop out if the first session feels like a monologue from the leader.

One valuable thing to do in this first meeting is to let group members tell a brief history of themselves. This could involve a handful of facts about where they come from and how they ended up in this group.

Also, in your first or second meeting, ask group members to share their expectations. The discussion may take the greater part of a meeting, but it's worth the time invested because it will help you understand each person's perspective. Here are some questions for initiating a discussion of group members' expectations:

- How well do you expect to get to know others in the group?
- Describe your previous experiences with small groups. Do you expect this group to be similar or different?
- What do you hope the group will be like by the time the study ends?
- How do you think this group will contribute to your walk with Christ?
- Do you need to finish the meeting by a certain time, or do you prefer open-ended meetings? Do you expect to complete this study in ten sessions, or will you be happy extending it by a few sessions if the additional time serves your other goals for the group?

If you have an extended discussion of people's expectations, you probably won't actually begin session 1 of this study guide until the second time you meet. This is more likely if your group is just forming than if your group has been together for some time. By the time you start the first session in the study guide, group members ought to be accustomed to interacting with one another. This early investment will pay big dividends. If you plan to take a whole meeting (or even two) to lay this kind of groundwork, be sure to tell the group what you're doing and why. Otherwise, some people may think you're simply inefficient and unable to keep the group moving forward.

Remember that many people will feel nervous during the first meeting. This is natural; don't feel threatened by it. Your attitude and demeanor will set the tone. If you are passive, the group will lack direction and vision. If you are all business and no play, they will expect that the group will have a formal atmosphere, and you will struggle to get people to lighten up. If you are all play and no business, they will expect the group to be all fluff and won't take it seriously. Allow the group some time and freedom to form a "personality." If many group members enjoy a certain activity, join in with them. Don't try to conform the group to your interests. You may have to be willing to explore new activities.

What does the group need from you initially as the leader?

- *Approachability:* Be friendly, ask questions, avoid dominating the discussion, engage with group members before and after the sessions, allow group members opportunities to ask you questions too.

- *Connections:* Pay attention to how you can facilitate bonding. (For example, if you learn in separate conversations that two group members, Joe and Tom, went to State University, you might say, "Joe, did you know that Tom also went to State U?")

- *Communication of Logistics:* Be simple, clear, and concise. (For instance, be clear about what will be involved in the group sessions, how long they will last, and where and when they will occur.)

- *Summary of Your Leadership Style:* You might want to put together some thoughts about your style of leadership and be prepared to share them with the group. You might include such issues as:

  1. The degree of flexibility with which you operate (for example, your willingness to go on "rabbit trails" versus staying on topic)

  2. Your level of commitment to having prayer or worship as a part of the group

  3. Your attentiveness, or lack thereof, to logistics (making sure to discuss the details surrounding your group, such as when and where you are meeting, or how to maintain communication with one another if something comes up)

  4. The degree to which you wear your emotions on your sleeve

  5. Any aspects of your personality that have often been misunderstood (for instance, "People sometimes think that I'm not interested in what they are saying because I don't immediately respond, when really I'm just pondering what they were saying.")

  6. Any weaknesses you are aware of as a leader (for example, "Because I can tend to dominate the group by talking too much, I will appreciate anybody letting me know if I am doing so." Or, "I get very engaged in discussion and can consequently lose track of time, so I may need you to help me keep on task so we finish on time.")

  7. How you plan to address any concerns you have with group members (for instance, "If I have concerns about the way anyone is interacting in the group, perhaps by consistently offending

another group member, I will set up time to get together and address it with that person face-to-face.")

- *People Development:* Allow group members to exercise their spiritual gifts. See their development not as a threat to your leadership but as a sign of your success as a leader. For instance, if group members enjoy worshiping together and you have someone who can lead the group in worship, encourage that person to do so. However, give direction in this so that the person knows exactly what you expect. Make sure he or she understands how much worship time you want.

Beginning the Sessions

Before you jump into session 1, make sure that group members have had a chance to read "A Model of Spiritual Transformation" beginning on page 9 and "A Method for the Biblical Exercises" beginning on page 17. Also, ask if they have done what is listed in the "Preparation" section of session 1. Emphasize that the assignments for each session are as important as the group meetings and that inadequate preparation for a session diminishes the whole group's experience.

Overview of *Ministry*

This study is designed to motivate and direct believers into a life of ministry. Ministry is the calling of every follower of Christ. This study will help those who have never considered their life as a ministry, as well as those who need to refine their current ministry efforts. Christians are people who have been marked by an experience of Christ's love. As a result, they ought to live out, increasingly as they mature, a commitment to love and serve others. That is what ministry is all about.

Life Vision

The *Ministry* study uses a tool called "Life Vision." "Life Vision" is a set of exercises that group members complete throughout the study. The exercises help group members (1) identify unique aspects about themselves;

(2) recognize the needs of others; (3) develop a vision for utilizing various talents, spiritual gifts, and resources to minister to the physical and spiritual needs of others; and (4) create a plan of action steps to attain their vision.

The Order of Sessions

This study's first two sessions are designed to give group members a theologically grounded motivation for ministry. In session 3, group members will identify the many different contexts of life in which ministry can occur. Session 4 provides a reminder and a sort of warning against pursuing ministry endeavors without the guidance and strength of God's Spirit. The next three sessions walk the group through, in more detail, a discussion of ministry in each major context of life: the world, the church, and the home. The corresponding "Life Vision" exercises will guide group members through the process of identifying action steps for ministry in each context. The climax of the study is the "Life Vision" presentation. Over the course of sessions 8–10, individuals share their visions for ministry in the world, the church, and the home, as well as a plan for living them out. The study concludes with a worship-oriented discussion about how ministry glorifies Christ in the world.

Discussion Questions

This "Leader's Guide" contains questions that we think will help you attain the goal of each session and build community in your group. Use our discussion questions in addition to the ones you come up with on your own, but don't feel pressured to use all of them. However, we think it's wise to use some of them. If one question is not a good vehicle for discussion, then use another. It can be helpful to rephrase the questions in your own words.

Session 1: Expanding Your Concept of Ministry

At least a week before you discuss session 1, meet with your group to introduce the study and make sure people know how to complete the "Personal Inventory, Part I" exercise as well as the biblical exercise. The homework for this session is longer than for most other sessions, so prepare your group for that. If necessary, you could expand this session into two, or you could let some members skip the biblical exercise.

The goal of session 1 is to leave each person with a new or renewed understanding of ministry as an all-pervasive part of the Christian life. Make sure group members understand the definition of ministry in the session content. Use the following questions to instigate discussion:

1. Is the notion that you are called to minister a new concept for you? If yes, how does it make you feel? If no, in what ways is your life a life of ministry?

2. Share about others who have ministered to you by being "others-oriented." What did they do to minister to you?

3. What does the 1 Peter passage say about having an others-orientation? How does a "pagan" lifestyle contrast with a ministry lifestyle as described in this passage? What habits do you have, because of personal preferences or the influence of friends or culture, that hinder you from having an others-orientation?

4. In the routines of your daily life, how are you currently expressing an others-orientation?

5. In what area of your life do you most need to grow in thankfulness? In integrity? In wholeheartedness?

6. Do you know what your spiritual gifts are? Have you found outlets in the church for expressing your gifts? If so, what has your experience been like?

Make sure group members understand how to complete the "Personal Inventory, Part II" exercise.

Session 2: Ours for Others

This session challenges group members to see that they are called to minister. Much of your discussion ought to revolve around the phrase "Ours for others." The following questions are designed to help individuals see what resources they have been given (see parts I and II of "Personal Inventory") and consider how they can use those resources to serve others.

1. When you looked back over your list of the abilities, spiritual gifts, interests, character, and material possessions that God has given you or developed in your life, what surprised you?

2. What resources had you not given much thought to in relation to serving others?

3. What resources do you struggle to use in service to others?

4. Why do you have a hard time using those resources in service to others?

Make sure group members understand how to complete the "Roles and Needs" exercise.

Session 3: Contexts of Ministry

This session introduces the idea of seeing ministry in light of three major life contexts: the world, the church, and the home. The discussion should enable group members to share the needs they identified in the "Roles and Needs" exercise. Consider asking these questions:

1. Did you struggle to identify others' needs in your various contexts?

2. How can we as a group help you identify some needs in those contexts?

3. What needs did you identify that you had not previously recognized?

4. What needs did you identify that you feel powerless to address? Why do you feel powerless?

5. What needs have you tried to meet and then failed? Why have your attempts failed?

6. How aware are people of the needs you have tried to meet?

7. Should we always start by meeting the felt needs of others? Why, or why not?

8. How does meeting a felt need provide opportunities to meet spiritual needs?

The purpose of several of these questions is to help the group see that while ministry is about more than meeting temporal needs, it often begins with temporal needs. Ministry is more than meeting spiritual needs, though those needs are ultimately what we want to address.

Remind the group to do the "Ministry Vision Statement" exercise in session 4. This is a hard exercise for many people. Reassure the group that this is a rough draft of their vision statements. They will get a chance to revise their vision statements in future sessions. Also, note that these vision statements are secondary. The primary vision of every believer is to glorify Christ. These vision statements are the specific ways a believer tries to glorify Christ.

Session 4: Spirit-Directed Ministry

The goal of this session is to remember that because service in the flesh falls short of our goal, our ministry needs to be by the power of the Spirit. Using these questions, facilitate a discussion to help people see why dependence on God is essential in ministry:

1. What did you learn from John 15 about the Spirit's role in our efforts to serve others?

2. Describe an experience in your life when the Spirit directed you with His Word.

3. Describe an experience in your life when the Spirit directed you through the counsel of others.

4. Describe an experience in your life when the Spirit directed you through the desires of your heart.

5. How do you evaluate whether or not you are depending on the Spirit's guidance?

6. How do you evaluate whether or not you are maintaining an others-orientation?

7. Is it more important to you that you have maintained dependence on the Spirit in the past day or week, or in your present moment? What is the difference between the two ways of thinking?

Answer any questions about the "Action Steps, The World" exercise to be completed for the next session.

Session 5: Ministry in the World

The session will center on a group exercise. Use these two questions to introduce that exercise:

1. How do your personality, education, and past experience affect your ministry attitude in your workplace?

2. What are the greatest obstacles you face in having a ministry mindset in the world?

Group Exercise

In this exercise, group members will give feedback about each other's gifts and acts of service. As the leader, you may want to write down some notes about each member before the group session. Use some of the following questions to help you write down useful notes to share with each person:

1. In what ways are you aware that this person has served others in the world?

2. What have you noticed that he or she talks about regarding his or her workplace or other involvement in the world?

3. What strikes you as unique about his or her approach to fulfilling responsibilities in the world?

4. Given the person's workplace and other world settings, how do you think he or she could be an effective witness for Christ?

For the group exercise, have each member take a turn being the focus. Encourage group members to describe how they envision that person's ministry in his or her world. Stick to a schedule so that everyone gets about the same amount of feedback.

After the exercise, encourage the group members to review their ministry vision for the world and revise it with the feedback they received. Answer any questions about the "Action Steps, The Church" exercise to be completed for the next session.

Session 6: Ministry in the Church

This session will again focus on a group exercise. The following questions can be used for an introductory discussion:

1. How do your personality, education, and past experience affect the way you serve in your church?

2. What are the challenges you face in living out your ministry vision for the church? Or what challenges would you anticipate if you were to become involved in ministry in the church?

Group Exercise

Again, the goal here is to give each other feedback, this time about ministry in church or a Christian organization. For each person, have group members describe how they envision that person's ministry in the church or a Christian ministry. In preparation for the exercise, write down notes and questions for each group member before the group session. Use the following questions as you prepare useful notes about each group member:

1. How has he or she served others in the church?

2. What does he or she talk about regarding ministry in the church?

3. What strikes you as unique about his or her approach to ministry in the church?

4. Given the person's personality and background, what do you think are ways that he or she is or could be effective in ministry in the church?

After the exercise, encourage group members to review their ministry vision statements and revise them using the feedback they received. Remind them of the "Action Steps, The Home" exercise for next session.

Session 7: Ministry in the Home

This session works just like sessions 5 and 6. Use the following questions to warm up:

1. How do your personality, education, and past experience affect the ways you try to have a ministry in your home?

2. What are the greatest obstacles you face in living out your ministry vision for the home?

Group Exercise

You're going to give one another feedback as before, but this time for ministry in the home. In preparation for the exercise, use the following questions to write down notes about each of the group members:

1. In what ways has this person served his or her family?

2. What does he or she talk about regarding ministry to his or her family?

3. What strikes you as unique about his or her approach to ministry in the home?

4. Given the person's personality and background, how do you think he or she is or could be effective in ministry to family members?

After the exercise, encourage group members to review their ministry vision statements and revise them using the feedback they received. Ask them if they have any questions about the "Life Vision" presentations. Determine and relay the order in which members will give their presentations over the next several sessions.

Sessions 8–10: Life Vision Presentations

You may decide to do your "Life Vision" presentation first as an example. On the other hand, it may be helpful for you to arrange for another group member to go first so you can demonstrate the kinds of responses you expect. After each person shares, ask clarifying questions, offer appreciation, and give encouragement. Ask the person if there is any way that the group can support or partner in his or her ministry vision. Finally, take time for the group to pray for that person's vision for ministry.

Make sure people limit their presentations to fifteen minutes each. Limit feedback to ten minutes per presenter. In this way you can get through three or four presentations during each meeting.

Session 11: For the Glory of Christ

Use the following questions to spur on discussion:

1. What would be the impact in a company if ministry-minded Christians were scattered throughout the organization, from the top leadership down to the lowest-paying position? How would Christ be glorified?

2. What would your church be like if all of the members got involved in ministry? When visitors came to a church event, what would they observe? How would Christ be glorified?

3. What would be the impact on a community if all the families in your church body had a ministry mindset? How would that affect neighborhood gatherings, Little League games, school events, and birthday parties? How would Christ be glorified?

Provide closure to the study by having group members talk about how the study has changed their perspective of ministry. Use the following questions:

1. In what ways do you see your life differently as a result of this study?

2. How did this study change your understanding of God? How did it change your understanding of the Christian life?

3. How did this study help you follow the command to love God and love people?

Conclusion

We hope this study has been helpful for you and your group members. We desire to provide materials that help believers grow in Christ through small-group communities. Don't hesitate to contact us if you have any questions!

Phone: (214) 841-3515
E-mail: sf@dts.edu

Notes

A Method for the Biblical Exercises

1. Howard G. Hendricks and William D. Hendricks, *Living By the Book* (Chicago: Moody, 1991), p. 166.

Session 1: Expanding Your Concept of Ministry

1. Martin Luther, as quoted in R. Paul Stevens, *The Other Six Days: Vocation, Work, and Ministry in Biblical Perspective* (Grand Rapids, Mich.: Eerdmans, 1999), p. 77.
2. www.opc.org/documents/WSC_text.html
3. Robert Banks, *Redeeming the Routines: Bringing Theology to Life* (Wheaton, Ill.: BridgePoint, 1993), p. 29.
4. R. Paul Stevens, *The Other Six Days: Vocation, Work, and Ministry in Biblical Perspective* (Grand Rapids, Mich.: Eerdmans, 1999), p. 6.

Session 2: Ours for Others

1. R. Paul Stevens, *The Other Six Days: Vocation, Work, and Ministry in Biblical Perspective* (Grand Rapids, Mich.: Eerdmans, 1999), p. 88.
2. Os Guinness, *The Call: Finding and Fulfilling the Central Purpose of Your Life* (Nashville: Word, 1998), p. 29, emphasis added.
3. Guinness, p. 47, emphasis added.

Session 5: Ministry in the World

1. Walter Wangerin, Jr., "Hans Christian Andersen: Shaping the Child's Universe," in *Reality and the Vision: Eighteen Christian Authors Reveal What They Read and Why*, ed. Philip Yancey (Dallas: Word, 1992), p. 1.

OTHER BOOKS IN THE TRANSFORMING LIFE SERIES.

Identity

Pinpoint key elements of who you are—your heritage, roles, and distinctiveness—in Christ.
1-57683-558-8

Community

Explore what it takes to combat isolation and build true Christian community.
1-57683-559-6

Integrity

Identify ways to overcome the habits that are contrary to the values you profess as a Christian. Instead discover Christlike character traits you can develop and live out.
1-57683-561-8

To get your copies, visit your local bookstore, call 1-800-366-7788, or log on to www.navpress.com. Ask for a FREE catalog of NavPress products. Offer BPA.